South Africa

Reasons to Believe!

Guy Lundy

Wayne Visser

Foreword by Tim Modise

AARDVARK

Published by Aardvark Press
PO Box 37571
7978 Valyland
Cape Town
South Africa

**Aardvark Press is a Proudly South African enterprise.
Visit our website at www.aardvarkpress.co.za**

ISBN 0-9584564-1-0

First edition 2003

Design and setting by Aardvark Press
Cover design by Cornelle Ellis
Cover artwork by Rosalind Grey Stockhall
Proofread by Vanessa Rogers
Reproduction by The Image Bureau
Printed by Tandym Print, 25 Thor Circle, Viking Place, Thornton

To order **corporate-branded editions** of this book, please contact the publisher directly: publish@aardvarkpress.co.za

For **trade orders**, please contact Pearson Education, tel: (+27) 21 531 7750 or fax: (+27) 21 532 0056

Very few teams, companies or individuals ever achieve success if they start out with negative and pessimistic attitudes. The same is true of countries – and of South Africa. Too many South Africans have become fixated with the negative aspects of our society. It is accordingly most refreshing to see a book like *South Africa – Reasons to Believe* that presents a balanced picture of South Africa – one that acknowledges our enormous assets, achievements and successes without denying the very real challenges – like AIDS, poverty and crime – that confront us. If we focus on the positives we will, with time, overcome our problems – just as we have done so often in the past.

South Africa is the most wonderful, exciting and relevant country in the world – but it is a hard country with little time for whingers and armchair critics. The response to problems should not be to throw up one's hands in despair and to criticise from the sidelines. It should rather be to roll up our sleeves and to join one another in making our wonderful country a truly winning nation for all its people.

FW de Klerk, former President of South Africa

Every day, we at the International Marketing Council of South Africa are confronted by South Africans who want to make a difference, who see the potential in our country and who want to find ways to showcase our success to the world. We are proud to support initiatives, such as this book, which work towards creating a better country, which highlight the positive and which enable us all to believe that we live in a country *Alive with Possibility*.

Each one of us has a personal responsibility to create a vision for a better future and to go out of our way to try and make it happen. There is so much success waiting to be discovered here, so much that we can show the world as we work on improving our image, improving the lives of our people and encouraging tourism and investment. Our diversity, our energy and vibrancy are compelling to visitors to this country – let us all make a conscious effort to build, to improve our society, to enhance our unity and to seek out the positive. We are an inspiring nation, if only we can believe that!

Yvonne Johnston, Chief Executive Officer,
International Marketing Council of South Africa

South Africans must do more to market their country. Why be negative when there is so much to be positive about? Like many others, I am extremely hopeful about South Africa's future. That is why we at Unilever gave President Mbeki access, through the International Marketing Council, to our strategic brand-marketing model – so that we can all start to rebuild positive perceptions of South Africa. In a similar spirit, I welcome this book, which reminds South Africans of all the good reasons they have to believe in themselves and their country.

Sir Niall FitzGerald KBE, Chairman, Unilever plc

Making sense of South Africa is, as I see it, a two-eyed business. That so many people have been suckered into applying only one eye, the dismal eye, not only makes for dreary conversation, but also risks making a self-fulfilling prophecy. 'Hijackings!', they wail. 'Muggings! Poverty! Let's get our money out! And then follow it!' (To places where people once wailed 'Highwaymen! Footpads! Poverty!').

Thanks and congratulations to Guy and Wayne for prising open the public's other eye, the eye that sees successes, rewards, and the big stimulus of meeting big challenges. They restore a balance, and take us a strong step on the road to the upcoming attitude that says 'Yep, it's ours, we belong, let us celebrate what is great and fix what is not.'

Denis Beckett, writer and broadcaster

Key to all of South African Tourism's initiatives to market South Africa as a preferred tourist destination to the rest of the world must be entrenched in each and every South African the realisation that we indeed have many *Reasons to Believe* that we are well down the road towards a better future for all our citizens.

I am therefore delighted to have been asked to add my endorsement to this valuable publication that adds weight to the growing conviction that we are all Proudly South African. We can all feel justly proud in the wide range of truly world-class quality tourism products that South Africa has to offer, each of which adds tremendous value to its natural scenic beauty, culture, warmth and hospitality of our people in making South Africa a truly global tourist destination of choice.

It is only when we believe in ourselves, that other people will believe in us and tourism will be empowered to take its rightful place as one of the country's top five industries in its contribution to sustained economic growth, job creation and contribution to GDP.

Cheryl Carolus, Chief Executive Officer, South African Tourism

This book teems with examples that demonstrate our good fortune in living in this country. We have the talent, the diversity and the environment to rank with the best in the world. In a post-9/11 world, we are a model for the kind of reconciliation process required within the rich and the poor nations to make our planet sustainable.

**Clem Sunter, writer, speaker and
Chairman, Anglo American Chairman's Fund**

We live in a beautiful country with great resources – and the greatest resource of all is the people of our land. We performed a political miracle in the early nineties. I believe we now stand at the brink of an economic miracle where the frontiers of poverty will be rolled back and society uplifted. I am truly proud to be a South African and loved reading this book. It is magic!

Roddy Sparks, Managing Director, Old Mutual South Africa

Dedications

This book is dedicated to:

All those individuals and organisations whose belief in South Africa – its people and its potential – have made this country the great nation that it is today, and whose ongoing constructive action and enduring positive spirit, is our hope for the future.

The memory of my mother, who never stopped believing in her beloved country. If only she could be here to see it fully meet the potential that she always knew it had.

– Guy Lundy –

My parents, who taught me that we create our reality; my sister, who inspires me through her caring for others; my nephew, who is a child of the new South Africa; and my wife, who sustains me while I'm forever chasing rainbows.

– Wayne Visser –

A word of thanks ...

To Christine and Kathleen, for their unfailing support, patience and understanding;

To Proudly South African and the International Marketing Council of South Africa, for their timely encouragement and support;

To Tracey Whitelaw of Aardvark Press, for believing wholeheartedly in this book right from the start, and gently coaxing us to the end;

To KPMG and *morrisjones&co* for their support in launching the book;

To Geoff McDonald of Unilever in London for his contagious optimism and enthusiasm, and for the steady stream of good-news media coverage on South Africa;

To Pearson Education South Africa for their assistance in getting the book out there;

To *Fair Lady* and *Sawubona* magazines, the source of many of the inspiring stories featured in the book; and,

To the many others who passed positive information and encouragement our way.

Contents

Foreword

Tim Modise
Chairman of Proudly South African

This book is a celebration of what should be obvious, but isn't. It highlights facts about South Africa and stories of what South Africans have done which should form part of our common vocabulary, but which do not.

The authors have covered a wide spectrum of what South Africa has to offer – from the natural beauty of the South African landscape, to the impressive infrastructure; from economic achievements to business success stories; from sporting highs to our cultural heritage. What shines through most strongly is that behind all the achievements are people.

It is South Africa's people who have made, and who are making, the difference. Whether they are waitrons in restaurants, taxi drivers carrying tourists, lecturers and teachers educating the youth, activists involved in NGOs, senior business decision-makers or public servants, South Africans are the main reason why we should believe in South Africa.

The authors do not present a blind optimism. This book does not shy away from the challenges that face South Africa, one of the biggest being enormous wealth disparities. It does say, however, that those actively involved in doing something about the problems around them tend to be more optimistic, even though they are sometimes exposed to the most dire of circumstances. The fact that these two young businessmen have taken time out to find and write up the stories highlighted in this book, deserves our appreciation. They have made an important contribution towards building national pride.

Together, we can help ensure that the celebration of South Africa can be one that all its people can share. In the same way, we at Proudly South African also believe we are making a contribution, through promoting local goods and services. Companies producing quality goods, using fair labour standards and sound environmental practices can identify themselves with the Proudly South African logo, and individuals and companies wanting to do their bit for jobs and the economy can select those products and services.

I pledge allegiance

We believe that all South Africans – at home and abroad – face a critical choice. It is no small matter, this choice. In fact, it is a choice upon which the very future of our young nation rests. The well-being of millions of people depends on this choice. Your own individual happiness will be determined by this choice. No small matter, indeed!

So, here it is – the choice: either we *choose* to embrace South Africa with a positive, constructive and engaging spirit, or we *choose* to submit to pessimism, fear and misery. That's it. Nothing complicated really. It's a simple choice and yet it's a choice each of us has to make, and does make (consciously or unconsciously), every day.

There is no room for 'ifs' and 'buts', because the choice to be positive or negative has *nothing* to do with politics, the economy or crime. It has *everything* to do with our spirit, our heart, our attitude. Especially our attitude. In this 'cruel, crazy, beautiful' country that is South Africa, our attitude is the only thing that each of us has complete control over. Our attitude shapes our perception and our perception in turn shapes our reality. In this book, we want to challenge those who are choosing attitudes that hurt rather than heal, that destroy rather than create, that knock down rather than build up. We believe that their pessimistic attitudes are neither justified nor helpful – to themselves, to others, or to the country as a whole.

On the other hand, we know that there is a rising tide of people who are fed up with all the whinging and whining; people who can see the good that is going on but which is being ignored or perhaps under-reported by the media. These are people who want to get on and tackle the problems, rather than complain about them. They can see their own hand in shaping a better future for this country. Most of all, they feel something in their gut that is hard to explain – it is an emotion that wells up from deep inside every time they reflect on being South African.

We know that these people are out there because of the way in which the idea for this book came about in the first place. It began with the massive response from South Africans and others, living here and around the world, to a speech made by Guy, entitled 'I pledge allegiance'. The original speech was made at a Toastmasters meeting in Cape Town in October 2001, where it was very well received. However, its real power became evident when it was sent out to a few friends by e-mail … who sent it out to a few of their friends by e-mail … who sent it on … and on … and on. A whole new breed of e-mail virus! In the end, the speech was read by thousands of people from places as far-flung as Australia, Hong Kong, Kuwait and the USA. They didn't just read it – it really pushed some buttons and the e-mails and phone calls and media interest started flooding in. The message was clear: people are thirsty for *reasons to believe*, to feel positive, in the midst of the desert of pessimism that pervades the South African mindscape.

Given its pivotal role as a catalyst for this book, we want to begin our virtual journey together by quoting that speech word for word. You may even recognise it as having found its way into your own e-mail in-box. Here it is:

"I pledge allegiance to the flag of the United States of America and to the Republic for which it stands, one nation under God, indivisible, with liberty and justice for all.' Many years ago I was an exchange student in the USA, and every morning in my school, as in all schools across America, all classes came to a halt as the Pledge of Allegiance came over the loudspeaker system and every student stood to repeat these words. I was quite amazed by this display of daily brainwashing in the so-called 'land of the free'. In hindsight it isn't actually that amazing, because we've all experienced how Americans are just so proud to be American! No matter how big their problems, and heaven knows they've got a lot of them, Americans will still spend hours telling you how fantastic their country is, and in fact how it is better than pretty much anywhere else in the world.

What a contrast then, when I later spent a few years in London, and I ended up actively avoiding other South Africans. Why? Because frankly their negativity about our homeland irritated me so much. These people, who will gladly put new South African flags on their cars and support a whole cottage industry importing biltong and NikNaks to munch on as they cheer the Springboks at Twickenham, will spend hours telling anyone who will listen just how awful it is in South Africa, how lucky they are to be in London, and how they are never going back because the country is in such a mess. At the time, I put it down to the fact that they were justifying why they were holed up in their dingy little flats under grey London skies, while their friends and family enjoyed the sunshine on Camps Bay beach.

However, when I came home, expecting to be greeted by the smiles of new South Africans everywhere, I was very disappointed to find that exactly the same attitude is pervasive right here. The number of people who asked me why I came back, and why on earth I had brought my French wife with me, simply amazed me. I would have thought the answer was perfectly obvious! I was later very disturbed, although not surprised, to hear that our President found it necessary to make a point to South African businessmen that they should stop running down their own country on overseas business trips. Can anyone tell me what it is that makes sense about running down your own home to foreign people that you would like to visit here and invest here? It seems to me like inviting your boss to dinner at your house in the hope of getting a promotion, but discouraging him from coming because you're a terrible cook and your dog bites.

Yes, we have problems, but so does everybody else. Sure, the rand is down the toilet, but if you look closely enough you'll see that just about every other emerging-market country has suffered from the same woes – and that includes Australia and New Zealand, which everyone seems in such a rush to get to. And aren't we lucky that we aren't living in Argentina with their currency crisis? Sure, our neighbour, Zimbabwe, is facing economic ruin and the ridicule of the developed nations, but man am I glad that I don't live in Pakistan right now. We have AIDS, and we also have an army of people trying to find a cure for it – possibly more vigorously than anywhere else, since we have the most to lose from it. We do have corruption, and the Americans have George W Bush, whether they like it or not. We've got all sorts of problems, yes, but must we be so hard on ourselves?

In many ways we are far better off in South Africa as a whole than we have been at any time in our history. Our people are getting educated and housed at a world-beating rate; we have amongst the world's cheapest electricity; our inflation is the lowest it's been in my lifetime; we have an economic growth rate; and there is development everywhere you look. We have so much going for us: we have so many good people, such an interesting mix of cultures; we have so much beautiful countryside and so many natural resources that we can draw from – we really have such a bright future ahead of us.

Let us concentrate on the positive things that surround us every day: the sunshine, the people, the beauty, the progress. Constantly criticising our country can only do harm – for you personally (your personal feeling of happiness and well-being), and for the country that you know from the bottom of your heart that you love, otherwise you wouldn't be here.

Ladies and Gentlemen, I implore you: do not run down South Africa, neither at home nor overseas. Become ambassadors of your country. Welcome foreign guests and point out how far we have come and how far we're going to go; how they need to watch out for us on the world stage. And if you're overseas on business or holiday (if you can afford it), tell people how much South Africa has going for it, and invite them to come and see for themselves.

I have devised my own pledge of allegiance and I'd like to repeat it to you now:

I pledge allegiance to the flag of the Republic of South Africa and to the interesting people, places and idiosyncrasies for which it stands, one nation under several religions, languages and cultures, yet indivisible, with freedom, basic needs and progress for all.

That is my pledge of allegiance to my home, our home. I pledge to help others see what is so good about South Africa. Join me in being positive about our country and about ourselves as South Africans. Let's get out there and spread the word so that we can eradicate negativity and replace it with a wave of positive, South African patriotism.'

Well, people really *did* get out there and spread the word, but the speech was just the spark. At the same time, a small group of visionary South Africans organised the country's first National Be Positive (B+) Day on 2 November 2001. It was a rallying cry that even President Mbeki took up. Then we were contacted by the Proudly South African organisation, which was just getting off the ground as one of the concrete outcomes of the 1998 Presidential Jobs Summit. Next, we were introduced to the Brand South Africa initiative – an initiative proposed by President Mbeki's International Investment Council, made up of international business leaders who recognise that South Africa needs an image overhaul. And so the fire continued to spread!

The interest in being positively South African was definitely heating up, and we sensed that it was part of something bigger. More than just a feel-good blitz, we were standing on the cusp of a turning point in attitudes. Malcolm Gladwell wrote a book called *The Tipping Point*, in which he compared the spread of 'social epidemics' such as the use of cell phones to the spread of any other epidemic. He pointed out that just as a single person can start a 'flu epidemic, so too can a small but precisely-targeted push start a social epidemic. We felt then (and still feel now) that South Africa is about to reach that tipping point. Perhaps we could add some fuel to the flames, and help push South Africans over the threshold? Then we might achieve a positive breakthrough in our collective enthusiasm and optimism about the future of this amazing country, and ourselves as South Africans.

And so the idea of our book was born. The essence of the book is in its title. There are so many 'reasons to believe' in the future of South Africa, and we want to help people here, and internationally, to see past the media fog of bad news to the good things that we can be proud and positive about. We have come so far from the days when books like Alan Paton's *Cry the Beloved Country* encapsulated what it really meant to be South African. We can now celebrate what we have achieved and be hopeful about what lies ahead.

In the chapters to come, we take a look at the mood swings that South Africa has endured in the past two decades, bringing us up to the present day and the groundswell of new and exciting initiatives to rejuvenate our flagging spirits and re-brand our national image. Then we go on to explore numerous powerful reasons why we have every right to feel both positive and proud about South Africa. We conclude with what we can *do*, collectively and as individuals, to turn the potential of this country into a living reality.

'I pledge allegiance to the flag of the Republic of South Africa and to the interesting people, places and idiosyncrasies for which it stands, one nation under several religions, languages and cultures, yet indivisible, with freedom, basic needs and progress for all.'

We hope that, as you read this book, you too will have cause to smile with confidence and to feel the warm glow of contentment that *we* feel about being South African. Not to mention the blazing passion for this country and its people! Working together, we can continue to transform South Africa, cast light on our shadowed continent, and inspire the world to become a better place.

Ten top *Reasons to Believe* in South Africa

1. **SA is a nation of survivors.** We've transformed countless times and faced untold hardships with great courage and remarkable endurance. We've got tried-and-tested skills to *vasbyt*, to adapt, to survive, to thrive.

2. **SA is proof that miracles do happen.** Between 1994 and 2001, people with houses increased from 64 per cent to 77 per cent, people with electricity went up from 58 per cent to 80 per cent and those with piped water rose from 68 per cent to 76 per cent.

3. **SA is rapidly redefining its image.** From *morrisjones&co's* Homecoming Revolution ad campaign to expats, to Proudly South African's logo for quality local products, to the IMC's Brand South Africa initiative, 'Alive with Possibility'.

4. **SA is poised for an economic take-off.** We're currently the seventh best performing economy in the world with the third highest export growth rate (higher than the export explosion Japan experienced in the '50s and '60s!)

5. **SA inspires world-class business.** SABMiller is the world's second largest brewer, while the inspirational Mark Shuttleworth captured forty per cent of the Internet digital certification market before selling Thawte Verification for $575 million.

6. **SA is blessed with natural and cultural assets.** We have four World Heritage Sites: The Cradle of Humankind, Robben Island, St Lucia Wetland, and the Drakensberg. And the new 35 000 km^2 Great Limpopo Transfrontier Park is larger than many European countries.

7. **SA's diversity is a fountain of creativity.** Miriam Makeba was the first African Grammy winner in 1967. Nadine Gordimer won the Nobel Prize for Literature in 1991. Athol Fugard is the second most performed playwright in English after Shakespeare.

8. **SA has produced icons of history.** We have four Nobel Peace Prize winners – Albert Luthuli (1960), Desmond Tutu (1984), and Nelson Mandela and FW de Klerk (1993). Gandhi first tested his passive resistance technique in SA and Jan Smuts wrote the preamble of the UN Charter.

9. **SA can show the world a new better way.** No country is better positioned to prove to international onlookers that different cultures can co-mingle and produce a remarkable civilisation.

10. **South Africans can make a real difference.** Challenges bring opportunities to really do something meaningful. As Rabbi Warren Goldstein puts it: 'Our lives are full of significance here. It may not always be 'pleasantville', but it's always 'meaningful'.'

1 Storm clouds and rainbows

Weathering the change

There are many words to describe South Africa's incredible journey through recent history. 'Dull' is certainly not one of them; neither is 'boring' or 'predictable'. Rather, words like 'epic' and 'revolutionary' come to mind. Much like those brave and sometimes arrogant navigators and explorers of the New World, we South Africans are a travel-hardened and weather-beaten bunch, with many rough storms and cruel twists of fate behind us. Amazingly, we have endured. We are survivors. We should constantly remind ourselves how tough we really are; how, despite all the trials and tribulations we have faced, we have, repeatedly, overcome.

Of course, it's easy to be philosophical during the good times, when the sun is shining brightly and the waters are calm and sparkling. It's far more difficult when the wind is howling and the ship's mast is creaking; when the waves are crashing over the bows and the senses are numb from the lashing rain. And yet, this is exactly what the last few decades in South Africa have felt like – a relentless cycle of storms and rainbows. Like a sailing ship on the high seas, we have ridden out deep, dark troughs of fear and intimidation, going on to ride high on the crests of liberating change, only to be plunged back into the tempest again. It has been a rough ride by anyone's reckoning, and the journey is not yet at its end.

Perhaps it is not surprising, then, that fear and uncertainty still hang like a dark cloud over our national psyche. We acknowledge this bad-weather pessimism that many people feel in our country today, but it needs to be put into perspective. Here in our first chapter, as we briefly recall some of the highs and lows of our roller-coaster ride of recent years, we take heart from how far we have come in such a short time. After all, in the broad sweep of history, our achievements are nothing short of incredible. We remind ourselves how good we are at surviving and thriving, despite the odds. We are proof that the sun always does come out after the storm. We show that even the darkest clouds on our horizon have a silver lining. And, for good measure, we buff up those breathtaking colours of our rainbow nation.

Dark and gloomy days – 1985 to 1988

Let's face it – the threatening grey clouds had been building up steadily in the distance for some time before the storm eventually broke. The gold boom that propped up our economy at the height of the apartheid era was not a pot at the end of the rainbow after all. Its seductive lustre conveniently blinded the ruling nationalist government and its complicit white electorate to the shameful racism it had institutionalised.

The rest of the world saw things much more clearly; quite simply, that South Africa was rushing headlong into a bloody civil war. The way we look at the Israel-Palestine conflict and shake our heads today, is the same way that most of the international community looked at us then, with an overwhelming sense of hopelessness and desperation. Do you remember those dark days, in 1985, when President PW Botha (alias 'Die Groot Krokodil'), licked his lips, wagged his finger and made that disastrous Rubicon speech, in which he dismissed the world's criticism with a pat on his own back and a warning that they must 'not push us too far'?

Gloomy days indeed, as we continued to deny the majority of the population the basic right to vote and the nation suffocated in the icy grip of a political state of emergency with its iron fist of draconian censorship laws. As international isolation descended like a shroud over South Africa in the late 1980s, multinationals packed up and left, foreign direct investment dried up, the cultural boycott cut us off from the world stage of sports and arts, and anti-apartheid demonstrations gained momentum, both inside the country and abroad. Detention without trial, military conscription, flying bricks, flaming tyre 'necklaces', tear-gas police assaults, crippling labour strikes – the memories of that period of spiralling anarchy still have the power to haunt.

By the time Anglo American business leader, Clem Sunter, crystallised South Africa's future into 'high road' and 'low road' scenarios, few believed that the high road was anything more than a wishful fantasy. Nevertheless, we stood fast through the mayhem. We survived to tell the tale.

Rays of hope – 1989 to 1990

We can be eternally grateful that the prophecies of profound global transformation manifested themselves ten years before the new millenium. Perhaps the dramatic upheaval and sweeping changes in the world in late 1989 – the fall of communism, as the USSR broke up and the Berlin Wall came crashing down – ultimately helped to save South Africa from itself. As FW de Klerk ousted the ailing PW Botha as president, there was a miraculous break in the clouds and almost blinding rays of hope began to shine. The ANC and other revolutionary organisations were unbanned, apartheid laws were abolished and political prisoners were freed, including the icon of the struggle, Nelson Mandela. Who can forget his release from Victor Verster Prison – free at last, after more than 27 years!

Millions of South Africans and anti-apartheid activists from around the world rejoiced; many danced in the streets. Promises of re-investment started to flood in. There was excitement in the air – a frisson of nervous energy flowed through the land. Most of us felt a bewildering mixture of emotion – we were amazed and happy and cautious and uncertain, all at the same time. All in all, whatever our past prejudices, in the heart and soul of our being, we knew that these were good times. For the first time, it really looked like we might rescue ourselves from the gaping jaws of death into which we had been staring for so long as a country. Perhaps we might even make the transition relatively peacefully and safely. The 'high road' scenario suddenly started looking not only do-able, but desirable as well. Finally, after so many years of fighting and skulking and apologising and campaigning, we were all openly proud to be South African – what a feeling!

'I'm black and I'm proud of who I am, now that I've got back my dignity, thanks to our leaders.'

***Yvonne Chaka-Chaka
South African singer***

Storms of chaos – 1991 to 1993

The bubble soon burst. The South Africa that Mandela and his comrades returned to from incarceration and exile was not a peaceful one. After decades of political skullduggery, indoctrination and violence, the divisions and mistrust between the people of our country were massive. The gaps between black aspirations and white fears were all too obvious. Not surprisingly, suspicion was the order of the day. Even as the courage and wisdom of our political leaders – most notably De Klerk, Mandela, Cyril Ramaphosa and Roelf Meyer – steadily nudged us towards a negotiated settlement, our society was being torn apart at the seams.

Political jostling and public mud-slinging between the parties in the 'Codesa' talks spilled over into violence between the Inkatha Freedom Party and ANC members in Natal and the townships surrounding Johannesburg. Added to this explosive cocktail was the mysterious 'third force' (later linked to conservative right-wing groups) that aimed to wreak general havoc and set the black political groups against one another. As progress towards democracy continued unabated, the desperation of the old guard increased. ANC leader, Chris Hani, was assassinated and the country teetered on the brink of civil war again. As if to fan the flames, there was a disasterous attempt by the neo-nazi AWB group to prop up the Mangope regime in the homeland state of Bophutatswana.

While we were tossed around in the violent storms of change, chaos alone seemed to rule supreme. Many, especially the insecure white population, felt like they had been painfully and unceremoniously dumped from the dizzy heights of their initial wave of hope. Fears of 'another Zimbabwe' began to mount; so too did the white tide of mass emigrations, and the term 'brain drain' became a part of our everyday vocabulary. Most of those who took such rapid flight from our newly liberated shores proceeded to justify their choice by spreading disaster scenarios about the future of South Africa to all who would listen – and many did. (Many still do.) But the vast majority of South Africans gritted their teeth and got on with living here. We endured, again.

The sun comes out – 1994 to 1996

Fortune favours the brave and so it was with our eventual transition to democracy. The predictions of doom and destruction never materialised and April 1994 came knocking. We don't deny that those were tense times, as bombs exploded in a last-ditch effort by the 'third force' to avoid the inevitable, and the paranoid minority barricaded their houses and stocked up on tinned foods and bottled water. However, on the day itself – election day – in peaceful queues that snaked for miles, an overwhelming feeling of relief and happiness and pride in being South African returned with a vengeance. How far removed this was from the holocaust that had been predicted by the eternal pessimists.

The 'rainbow nation' (a term coined by Archbishop Desmond Tutu) was a fitting image for our political miracle and the promise of a brighter future. In fact, in the years that followed, South Africa didn't seem to be able to do anything wrong. In 1995, the country held its breath as Joel Stransky kicked the drop goal that took us to glory as Rugby World Cup champions, and tears of pride flowed as Mandela donned a number six Springbok rugby jersey in a victory salute to the nation. We came desperately close in the Cricket World Cup that year too, as we blamed the rain in Australia for robbing us of our place in the final. Then we won the Soccer

African Cup of Nations, which boded well for our international comeback at the next Soccer World Cup. Success breeds confidence, so we even decided to bid to host the 2004 Olympic Games in Cape Town. For a sports-mad nation, these were extremely powerful events. We felt like we were flying again.

Off the sports field, our charismatic political and sports leaders had earned the respect of the world and the passionate support of our nation. Nelson Mandela, FW de Klerk, Desmond Tutu, Tokyo Sexwale, Francois Pienaar, Hansie Cronje – here were people who couldn't help but buoy our spirits and make us feel that it was all going to be okay. International recognition followed and national pride swelled when Mandela and De Klerk jointly won the Nobel Prize for Peace. At the same time, our colourful new flag began to work its magic. We hadn't forgotten the enormous problems that South Africa still faced as a country – the poverty, unemployment, shortage of housing, lack of amenities, crime, HIV/AIDS and countless other challenges – but we were happy to ignore them for the time being, while we basked in the light of our own brilliance.

The rainbow fades – 1997 to 2001

You would think we would have learned from our previous sojourns through the peaks and valleys, but the national mood swung again when it became clear that the massive social and economic problems were not simply going to be wished away. We hit the ground with a hard bump (again) as the old realities, as well as some new ones, made their presence felt in many highly-publicised and confidence-crushing ways.

On the sporting front, which South Africans unwisely seem to take as a barometer for 'life, the universe and everything', matters seemed to get progressively worse. We lost our bids to host the Olympic Games and Soccer World Cup, while our rugby-winning streak came to an abrupt end and Springbok captain, Francois Pienaar, was given the boot. Then we were devastated when national cricket captain, Hansie Cronje, disgraced the country with his match-fixing scandal, and we got thoroughly beaten at the Soccer World Cup in France in 1998.

On the political front, Nelson Mandela's retirement had the financial markets in jitters, despite the ample capability and intellectual prowess of his successor, Thabo Mbeki. The 'Madiba magic' was always going to be a tough act to follow, but Mbeki's stances on such issues as HIV/AIDS and Zimbabwe, did little to endear him to the media or the masses. Other highly-respected and charismatic political leaders, such as Tokyo Sexwale and Cyril Ramaphosa, threw in the political towel and headed off to empower themselves economically in the boardrooms of big business, while Winnie Madikizela-Mandela continued to embarrass and irritate many with her scandalous antics.

The dent in our national ego was deepened by a string of high-profile fraud and corruption cases during the nineties, which included ANC stalwart and clergyman Alan Boesak's conviction for embezzling anti-apartheid donations, Tony Yengeni's alleged Mercedes 4x4 bribe acceptance in a R43-billion arms deal, and the collapse of the Health & Racquet Club group, through directors misappropriating funds. It didn't help that the primary listings overseas of the country's biggest businesses, such as Anglo American, South African Breweries, Old Mutual and Dimension Data, were interpreted by many as a vote of 'no confidence' in the South African economy. Nor that the rand plummeted against other major currencies in the 1999 emerging-market crisis. National depression set in almost visibly as the Reserve Bank's attempts to prop up the rand by raising interest rates to around 24 per cent failed to protect the currency from further speculative attacks, and culminated in 2001 lows of R13.85 to the dollar.

Dinner-talk blues

In many ways, the stormy ride we have just recounted is not dramatically different from the experiences of countless other developing countries in their post-liberation phase, but it was enough to keep the South African public and media moping in the gloomy troughs of a countrywide depression. In fact, it was during this period that pessimism started to become something of a national pastime. Each successive 'war story' recounted at dinner parties seemed to be topped by another more spectacular one.

The path of least resistance

Why is this? Are there some underlying reasons for our current malaise of negativity? Of course, we all know, it is easier to criticise than to be constructive, to complain rather than compliment and to break down rather than build up. So, in that sense, being negative is the path of least resistance. It takes no imagination or effort to run down the country.

More than this, the majority of people hate change. Tests by American psychologists, Holmes and Rahe, show that the most stressful events in life are virtually all related to change – things like divorce, retrenchment, retirement, fluctuations in finances, new work, and even taking a holiday. They point out that exposure to high levels of stress over a period of time can lead to anxiety, depression and pessimism. It's not difficult to spot the link with our South African condition, where radical change has been the rule rather than the exception over the past ten years or more.

Likewise, people fear the unknown. Although this is a survival mechanism that forces us to be cautious in the face of potential danger, it can also work against us when negative projections of the future become self-fulfilling prophecies. The lack of predictability or a positive direction in South Africa is no doubt one of the drivers of the pessimism that exists today. People have made their own assumptions to fill the gaps in their knowledge, backing them up with what they are told by others and what they see in the media. The overwhelming negativity of what they hear in turn only fuels their fears.

Another dimension of coping with 'unknowns' is the fact that apartheid was very effective in keeping blacks and whites apart in South Africa; hence, ignorance about others' cultures and lifestyles entrenched our false fears. This persists even today. After all, how many white people go to a black friend's home for dinner or a party, and vice versa? To illustrate the point further, Muzi Kuzwayo's book *Marketing Through Mud and Dust* was written specifically to help mostly white advertising executives better understand the black people to whom they are trying (often unsuccessfully) to market their products and services.

'Our lives are full of significance here. It may not always be 'pleasantville', but it's meaningful.'

Warren Goldstein
South African rabbi

The indoctrination and prejudice that we have been subjected to throughout our lives in South Africa is very difficult to shake off, especially for those of us who never went to multiracial schools or who were subject to daily brainwashing during the previous regime's compulsory military service. This helps to explain, but not excuse, many white South African's lack of belief in the competence of their fellow black South Africans. In the face of empowerment and affirmative action, many whites also feel that they have been unfairly pushed aside; hence, they tend to nurse their own egos by finding fault with their 'affirmative replacements'.

Our insistence on comparing ourselves to the UK, Europe or the USA also doesn't help. Although we have never been a First World country, we constantly use the developed world as our benchmark. We have so much more in common with our real competitors on the international playing field, such as Brazil, Mexico,

India, Pakistan, Australia, New Zealand, Egypt and Morocco. Unrealistic comparisons with highly-industrialised nations only serve to exacerbate our pessimism when we can't live up to the inappropriate expectations that these create.

So although we are poised at the crest of a wave, with everything in place to surf the transformation needed in this country, we are instead talking ourselves down into a stormy trough again. We shake our heads as we read the next depressing front-page news story and talk about it constantly with our friends at braais and dinner parties, reinforcing each others' feelings of doom and gloom. These dinner-talk blues are consistently dominated by a handful of issues, cited as reasons why some people do *not* believe in South Africa and its future. The four most prevalent of these are crime and corruption, HIV/AIDS, Zimbabwe, and the rand. So, we'd like to tackle these head-on, right here, upfront. While we don't want to downplay their seriousness as problems, we do also want point out that each of these clouds does have a silver lining.

Turning the tide on crime

Crime and corruption, at any level, is unacceptable. Full stop. In South Africa, the levels are worryingly high; certainly, in general, higher than in most First World countries. Rape and child abuse, in particular, as well as other violent crimes, are shockingly prevalent. Our police force has traditionally been poorly trained and underpaid. Our courts are bogged down and overloaded. Our jails are overcrowded and have become universities of crime, sometimes exacerbated by corrupt officials. We don't deny these things and we definitely don't endorse the situation, but we also don't lose our perspective on the issue.

One of the favourite sweeping statements of the pessimists is that South Africa has the highest crime rate in the world, or that our cities are the murder capitals of the world. This is simply not true. According to the United Nations, Colombia has the highest rate of intentional homicide per 100 000 people, Australia has the highest burglary rate, Spain has the highest robbery rate, and Norway has the highest rate of drug offences. Homerton Hospital in the London district of Hackney treats more gunshot and knife wounds per capita each month than the Chris Hani Baragwanath hospital in Soweto. Almost twice as many cars are stolen in Buenos Aires than in Johannesburg, three times more breaking and entering happens in Dar es Salaam, and twice as much robbery happens in Rio de Janeiro. However, debating where crime is worse is a pointless and futile exercise.

The question is, has our government and other institutions of society recognised the seriousness of crime in South Africa? Are they doing something about it? And are they winning the battle? The answer, in each case, is 'yes'. South Africa already has a relatively high number of police officers per capita. Compare our one police officer per 446 people with Denmark's one per 1 530 and the USA's one per 1 400. Even so, government plans to up our number to one per 389 people by 2006. That's even higher than the UK's one per 422. Furthermore, the state committed R8.4 billion to combating crime in the 2002 budget, a significant increase on previous years. This will go towards providing thousands more better-trained police officers on our streets and to solving crimes more effectively and efficiently. On many levels, the tide is already turning. For example, according to the 2001/2002 annual report of the South African Police Service, all but two of the twenty major crime categories either stabilised or improved during the period under review, compared to figures for previous years, since 1994. These included murder, commercial crime, shoplifting and motor-vehicle theft, which all decreased. Other categories like aggravated robbery, rape and housebreaking stabilised.

In 2001/2002, all but two of the twenty major crime categories either stablised or improved, compared with the years since 1994.

On the white-collar crime front, South Africa has its fair share, but we are not unique in this. Corruption scandals continue to rock political and business establishments the world over. Just think of the collapse of Enron and Worldcom and the almost daily allegations of corruption in the USA, UK and Europe, with some scandals reaching as high as the US Vice-President, the UK Secretary of Trade & Industry and the German Chancellor. What's more, South Africa has recognised the problem and is doing something about it, with initiatives ranging from the introduction of tougher legislation on money laundering, to the forfeiture of assets and proceeds of crime, to setting up improved government mechanisms such as the National Directorate of Public Prosecutions. The government has also committed to investigating areas of special concern, such as the Jali Commission on corruption in the prison system, and has created specialist FBI-style fraud-detection crack-squads, like the Scorpions Unit.

Again, we're not saying that things are yet at an acceptable level, but we are saying that the battle is being fought and there are signs that it is being won. We have no doubt that, in addition to the money and resources being ploughed into fighting crime directly, as the country's efforts at economic and social transformation continue to pay off, this will have a positive spin-off on crime alleviation as well.

What's positive about HIV/AIDS?

The HIV/AIDS pandemic is a human catastrophe of harrowing proportions, not just for South Africa, but for the whole world, and especially developing countries. A staggering five million people are estimated to be infected with HIV in South Africa, and the Medical Research Council predicts that between five million and seven million people will die of AIDS by 2010, leaving around two million AIDS orphans. As Clem Sunter concludes in a book about the subject, nothing short of a 'total onslaught' by every institution and sphere of society is required to halt the epidemic.

The important thing is not to become paralysed by the dire predictions. For instance, Iraj Abedian, chief economist at Standard Bank, is of the opinion that although the economic impact of HIV/AIDS on the South African workforce will be significant, it will not result in the 'economic catastrophe' some are touting. The problem *has* been recognised and action *is* being taken. Government, despite having wasted valuable time on esoteric arguments about whether or not HIV causes AIDS, has committed to increasing spending five-fold by 2004 – from R350 million in the 2001/2 budget to R1.8 billion in the 2004/5 budget. Most of this increase is expected to go into preventative education and research, in order to change people's behaviours and improve treatment options. In civil society, the awareness-raising work of organisations like loveLife and individuals like actor-satirist Pieter-Dirk Uys are making significant inroads into changing sexual behaviour. There was certainly evidence of a stabilisation in the HIV-infection rate in public antenatal clinics in South Africa between 1998 and 2001 .

Between 1998 and 2001 there was evidence of a stabilisation in the HIV infection found in pregnant women attending public antenatal clinics in South Africa.

At a corporate level, a positive precedent has already been set by a number of multinational organisations. For example, Boehringer-Ingelheim offered free Nevirapine to developing countries for five years to help stop mother-to-child HIV transmission. Furthermore, employers such as BP, BMW and Anglo American have set up HIV-treatment programmes, which include antiretroviral therapy for their HIV-positive employees and some or all of their families.

There are also inspiring examples of thousands of brave and compassionate individuals, some of whom we feature in this book, who are dedicated to making a difference when it comes to HIV/AIDS, whether it is by educating the youth, supporting those living with HIV, or caring for AIDS orphans.

So while HIV-related illness and the deaths caused by AIDS are going to put our country under a great deal of strain, both emotionally and economically, we shouldn't assume that the future is hopeless. The fact is that awareness and education *can* have a dramatic effect in reducing infection rates and treatment *can* prevent mother-to-child transmission. Drug therapy, albeit still incredibly expensive, *can* prolong by decades the lifespans, and improve the quality of life, of people living with HIV. So it is a war to be sure, but not one that *can't* be won.

Zimbabwe, the land of the setting sun

Robert Mugabe's style of politics is little short of dictatorial and the impact his policies are having on Zimbabwe is tragic. Like South Africa, Zimbabwe is a country of great promise, with the potential for being a highly-productive economy and a spectacular tourist destination. Especially when one considers that one of the positive outcomes of Mugabe's twenty-plus years in power, has been to improve general levels of education dramatically across the whole population. Alas, with his totalitarian politics, lack of press freedom, anti-West stance, condonement of land-invasions by so-called 'war veterans' and confiscation of white-owned farms, Zimbabwe has been brought to its knees, with inflation in triple-digits, a currency that is hardly worth the paper it is printed on, a rising tide of sanctions, and its people experiencing a widespread food crisis.

Zimbabwe's current course is not sustainable. As the pressure mounts, from the international community, from the vast majority of countries in Africa, and from the growing progressive population within the country itself, change *will* come – we think sooner, rather than later. Mugabe faced his toughest challenge yet from an opposition party in the presidential election of 2002. And it is a positive sign that it was South Africa's President Mbeki and Nigeria's President Obasanjo, who announced the suspension of Zimbabwe from the Commonwealth.

Of course, South Africa has borne the brunt of negative perceptions about Zimbabwe, especially by international investors and currency-market speculators, who tend to lump the whole region together in their analyses of the prospects for growth and prosperity. Some even go so far as to use Zimbabwe as a proxy scenario for South Africa's likely path of development. Many South Africans make the same grave, misinformed error of judgement. Yet there are fundamental differences between the histories, governments and economies of Zimbabwe and South Africa.

For example, when Zimbabwe changed political hands, the country was nowhere near as economically developed as South Africa is today. Zimbabwe had been torn apart by a bitter civil war, while South Africa changed hands relatively peacefully, after negotiation involving all parties. Rather than ignoring or covering up the past, the Truth and Reconciliation Commission helped South Africa to face up to its history and move forward in a positive spirit. The ANC, despite having had an armed wing, has throughout its ninety-year existence been primarily a political rather than a military organisation. It has a strong culture of democracy within its own ranks, and a deep commitment to promoting democracy within the country and on the African continent. South Africa's leadership role in the New Partnership for Africa's Development (NEPAD) is further proof of this.

On the emotive issue of property rights, any suggestion that white farmers in this country will suffer the same indignities as those in Zimbabwe ignores the South African government's firm stance *against* land-grabbing and its support *for* the sanctity of private ownership. South Africa has had a Land Claims Court in place for several years already, and the government is committed to completing the land-restitution process by 2005. Added to this is the trend of increasing numbers of South African farmers who are voluntarily helping to empower their workers through shareowner schemes, and by donating land and equipment to worker-run co-operatives.

In the southern African region, Botswana has had one of the highest sustained economic growth rates in the world and has the same debt rating as Japan.

It is also important for everyone, South Africans and foreigners alike, to remember that Zimbabwe is not our only neighbour. If investors want to judge our country by regional performance, they should take cognisance of the stable democracies and strong economic performances of Botswana, Namibia and Mozambique. Botswana in particular has had one of the highest sustained economic growth rates in the world for more than ten years, in the region of ten per cent per annum, and currently has the same debt rating as Japan. And Angola is already showing signs of flourishing, having brought years of bloody civil war to a virtual end. The weight of evidence showing the prospects for development in southern Africa is unquestionably positive.

The up-side of the falling rand

When the rand fell around 37 per cent against the US dollar during 2001, hitting a low of R13.85 to the dollar in December that year, the media went into a frenzy. The issue was seen by many as a national disaster, proof of South Africa's impending economic decline. In the media's sensationalist reporting style, any further weakening was termed a 'collapse', whereas any strengthening in the rand was referred to as 'gaining some ground'. Consequently, fluctuations in the exchange rate have become something of a barometer for the nation's mood swings.

We concede that any dramatic change in the economic environment of a country is not ideal. It damages business confidence, since stability is a prerequisite for effective forward planning. It also makes overseas travel, for those who can afford it, very expensive. In South Africa's particular case, at the end of 2001, the currency devaluation was attributed to a mixture of factors, including international instability after 11 September, speculative attack by financial market players, and negative perceptions of developing countries in general and southern Africa in particular.

However, it is important to put the rand-slide into perspective. Ours was not the only currency to experience a dramatic drop against the dollar during 2001 – Australia, New Zealand, Thailand, Venezuela, Brazil and other developing countries performed likewise. (As an aside, this also means that many of these countries are still relatively affordable for South Africans wishing to travel abroad.) Importantly however, the rand did not go into freefall. In the first months of 2002, it had already recovered over twenty per cent of its value against the dollar, making it the best performing currency in the world out of 56 currencies tracked by *Bloomberg News*. At the time of writing, the rand has already more than made up and is knocking on R9.00 to the dollar.

The silver lining surrounding the whole rand issue is actually an incredibly positive development. While it can and has led to inflation caused by increased prices of imports such as petrol, food and industrial components, the weak rand simultaneously makes the country extremely competitive as far as exports and tourism are concerned. Back in November 2001, even before the dramatic fall of the rand, Tradek economist Mike Schussler was quoted in *Business Day* as saying that, on the back of the weak rand, 'South Africa is experiencing a sustained export boom. South Africa's export explosion is bigger than what Japan experienced in the '50s and '60s, and this has been achieved without subsidies. This is a real export boom that would be welcomed as a miracle in other countries.' So why aren't we shouting this from the rooftops?

Likewise, during the first seven months of 2002, our weak currency was one of the factors that helped to lure more foreign tourists to South Africa than ever before – an increase of more than 236 000 extra tourists, 7.2 per cent more than over the same period the previous year. From Europe alone, the number of tourists increased by 16.2 per cent. Not surprising when you consider that, in July 2002,

Johannesburg was found by a global survey to be the cheapest major city in the world. It all helps.

So, rather than getting depressed about our weak rand, we should be scrambling to take advantage, so that we can fuel an ongoing recovery through increased Foreign Direct Investment (FDI) in our economy. FDI inflows, of course, require not only a competitive currency, but also positive perceptions on the part of investors. Which brings us back to the main theme of this book. South Africans and friends of South Africa have a critical role to play in building up the necessary levels of optimism

South Africa's export boom, achieved without subsidies, is larger than the boom that Japan experienced in the '50s and '60s.

about the country. This comes from being constructive about our own future, based on a balanced and factual assessment of our prospects, and communicating that positive attitude to the rest of the world. Thanks to several inspired initiatives, we have already gained a headstart on this front, as we will show in Chapter 3. But first, let's take stock of how far we have come since 1994, less than ten years ago.

2 Modern-day alchemists

In the quest for a magical formula for creating gold out of base metals, medieval alchemists mixed cocktails of seemingly incongruous ingredients. Their creative experimentation resulted in the discovery of an unprecedented number of chemical compounds that catapulted science and medicine forward. Similarly, South Africans have synthesised the diverse mixture of ethnic groups, languages, religions and cultures in our country and produced unexpected outcomes that seem, in some ways, magical.

When one compares our recent history to that of so many other nations that have undergone changes of similar magnitude, our success is almost inexplicable. We don't need to hail revolutionary war heroes like George Washington, Mao Tse Tung or Che Guevara here. Instead, we can celebrate four winners of the Nobel Peace Prize in as many decades – Albert Luthuli (1960), Desmond Tutu (1984), and Nelson Mandela and FW de Klerk (1993) – and a host of other harbingers of peace, hope and reconciliation. This chapter salutes these modern-day alchemists, the transformers of our society who, through their selfless contributions, have helped us to get to where we are today.

Talking heads and meeting minds

In South Africa, many of our original alchemists were in the political arena. In 1986, after the government imposed a State of Emergency, an increasing number of the political leaders of the day realised that there was no other sustainable way forward than to talk to their former number-one enemy, Nelson Mandela. Around the same time, Mandela had reached the same conclusion about the need for dialogue with the government. As a result, in 1987, a secret committee of senior government officials was formed to hold private discussions with Mandela about the future of the country. More or less in parallel, a select group of leaders from business and the Afrikaner establishment held a highly-publicised meeting with exiled leaders of the ANC in Dakar. After decades of misery, violence and suspicion, these were watershed events. People from across the political spectrum had realised that they needed to talk to each other if the country was to be saved from generations of bloodshed, and total ruin in the process.

The talks triggered a chain reaction of events leading to the dismantling of apartheid. In 1990, Nelson Mandela was released from prison and the ANC, and 33 other anti-apartheid organisations, were unbanned. More political prisoners were freed and exiles began to return home after as many as thirty years away. So began the arduous process of multiparty talks on the country's future. This process, called Codesa (which stood for 'Convention for a Democratic South Africa'), was in itself a remarkable achievement.

Codesa brought together eighteen delegations from across the political playing field. It was the largest gathering of different political groups that South Africa had ever experienced, although it was not the first time that South Africans had talked their way to a peaceful solution. (Between 1909 and 1910 whites managed to settle the differences which had fuelled the South African War and create the Union of South Africa, under Louis Botha and Jan Smuts.)

Codesa was by no means an easy or tidy process, but the political mudslinging and intense negotiations were infinitely preferable to the likely alternative of a civil war. The result of the talks was an agreement to draw up an interim Constitution and establish an elected assembly to draft a new, permanent Constitution. To ensure that the final Constitution embodied the principles agreed upon by the negotiators, a Constitutional Court was also established, consisting of eleven of the best legal experts in the country. If the new Constitution did not satisfy the agreed principles, the Court could send it back for redrafting – an arrangement that had never been seen anywhere else in the world.

Today we enjoy the benefits of the success of Codesa, and it is very easy for us to forget that rocky road to our country's first democratic election. Other nations, on the contrary, have not forgotten. They have taken note of South Africans' skills at coming to creative solutions in seemingly impossible circumstances. As a result, the same negotiators are in high demand to join peace missions and negotiating committees trying to break impasses in places like Northern Ireland, Israel and the Democratic Republic of Congo. Potential investors are also seeing how this spirit of negotiation continues in our country and consistently triumphs over inflexibility.

'X' marks the spot

Another outcome of the Codesa negotiations was the establishment of an Independent Electoral Commission (IEC) with the mandate to conduct elections at national and provincial level. Sixteen high-profile individuals, eleven local and five international, were appointed as commissioners to oversee the process and ensure that elections were free and fair. After much frantic preparation, the country's first democratic election was held on 26 April 1994 and continued until 29 April, to give everyone who wanted to vote the chance to do so, many for the first time in their lives.

Despite having to overcome logistical headaches, like inaccurate census figures and inadequate infrastructure in rural areas, the elections provided the world with some of history's most moving images: old ladies being taken to polling stations in wheelbarrows, beaming with pride; Afrikaner farmers and their workers standing side-by-side as they waited patiently for several days for the opportunity to make their crosses; and army helicopters delivering fresh ballot papers to mountainous areas that had run out.

South Africa is the only country in the world to have acquired, and subsequently fully dismantled, its nuclear-weapons capability.

The result of that first election was that the ANC won 63 per cent, the National Party twenty per cent and Inkatha eleven per cent of the poll of almost twenty million votes. For the first time, it clearly reflected the will of the majority of South Africa's people. There were no long, drawn-out attempts to declare the result invalid or go to war over what was seen as an unfair process. Instead, a Government of National Unity was established and it went to work immediately to draft the new Constitution.

By the time the second elections came around in 1999, things were quite different. The IEC, since established as one of six permanent state institutions supporting constitutional democracy, prepared and delivered the national and provincial elections in an unprecedented period of only thirteen months. After initial problems getting people to register as voters, the election itself ran so smoothly that international news agencies, hoping as always for something sensational to report on, actually described it as 'boring'. The IEC partnered with private-sector organisations to undertake monumental tasks, like developing a satellite-based Wide Area Network to 526 locations in only three months, creating the first comprehensive and accurate Geographic Information System in South Africa, and registering 18.4 million voters in 14 650 voting districts, in just nine days. The result was not only a smooth election, but also high praise and recognition through a host of international and national awards. These included America's prestigious Computerworld Smithsonian Award in 2000, for the powerful use of technology. All of the other four finalists for the award were American organisations. What a far cry from what had been predicted during our darkest days.

Turning wrongs into rights

Our fiercely-negotiated Constitution is one of the institutions that is now firmly in place to ensure that we don't go the way of countries such as India, Columbia or Zimbabwe which are regularly wracked by political violence and instability. After an initial adoption by the Constitutional Assembly on 8 May 1996, the Constitution was referred to the Constitutional Court for acceptance, which instead sent it back to Parliament for reconsideration. This in itself was a fascinating development – an independent panel of legal experts had rejected the new Constitution as not being totally in line with the spirit and principles of the new South Africa. The Court had already established its credibility amongst the political parties, the government and the public; hence the judges' decision was accepted more-or-less without question. The Assembly duly went back to redraft the non-compliant portions, and the new Constitution, with its Bill of Rights, was finally signed into law on 10 December 1996.

Today, our Constitution stands not only as one of the newest in the world, but it is also one of the most progressive. The process of writing it included the largest public-participation programme ever conducted in South Africa, involving intensive consultations with ordinary citizens, civil society and political parties. As a result, the Constitution has become a living document which exists to prevent repeat of the abuses of power and privilege that were so evident in the past. The general public has begun to take ownership of its rights, and has started to think in terms of government actions and policies having to be in line with the Constitution, and to challenge them if this appears not to be the case. Witness the examples of where government has been taken to court over policies relating firstly to the immigration of spouses of South African citizens and secondly the distribution of free anti-retroviral medication for HIV-positive pregnant women.

Critically, the rights of all South Africans are now protected by the Bill of Rights, which 'affirms the democratic values of human dignity, equality and freedom'. It includes rights to such essentials as adequate housing, freedom of expression and a clean environment, and it protects all citizens from abuses such as being deprived of their property, their children being used in armed conflict, or being detained without trial. No longer can the police, or anyone else, abuse these basic rights. In fact, like cops in the movies, our police are now required by law to promptly inform anyone they arrest of their 'right to remain silent' etc.

The Constitution and Bill of Rights are such a far cry from what existed, or more accurately, what did *not* exist, under the old dispensation. And yet people find it all too easy to forget how much better things are in comparison. Like the Americans do with their constitution, we need to learn to cherish and protect this new-found national asset of ours.

Forgive us our sins

Yet another of the wonders of South Africa's transition is the miracle of reconciliation. So often in the world's history of conquest, the victor has subjected the vanquished to the most terrible indignities – like the heavy penalties imposed upon Germany after the First World War, and the consequent rise of Hitler. Just as often, past wrongs have been virtually ignored, and the victims have been left to 'get over it' by themselves – as in the case of freed slaves after the American Civil War. South Africa after apartheid had the wisdom not to make either of these mistakes.

In 1995, the Promotion of National Unity and Reconciliation Act made provision for the establishment of a commission that would investigate gross violations of human rights that took place between 1960 and 1994, grant amnesty to perpetrators of those acts if they could show that they had been carried out with a political aim, and consider ways of making reparation to victims. The goal was to achieve reconciliation between perpetrators and victims, and to expose the details of what had happened, in the hope that our sensitised national conscience would prevent such tragic events from ever occuring again. The result was the Truth and Reconciliation Commission (TRC), headed by Anglican Archbishop Emeritus and Nobel Peace Prize winner, Desmond Tutu.

The TRC carried out its mandate by way of three committees. The Human Rights Violations Committee investigated the nature, extent and reasons for human rights abuses and, once it had established the identity and whereabouts of victims, passed the information over to the Reparation and Rehabilitation (R&R) Committee. The R&R Committee considered payment of reparations and support for victims, their families and their communities, where appropriate, to ensure that reconciliation was achieved and that the acts would never be repeated in the name of political ideology. The Amnesty Committee considered applications by the perpetrators of human rights violations to be freed from prosecution for the acts that they had committed.

The TRC was a very painful experience for everyone involved – the victims and their families, the perpetrators, the commissioners and the observers. Antjie Krog, the well-known Afrikaans author and poet who covered the proceedings for the SABC, described in her book, *Country of my Skull*, how everyone was either 'breaking down, cracking up or freaking out'. In the process, we found out a great deal about the apartheid propaganda machine too – how many South Africans were brainwashed and how terror was generated from within the establishment.

In the end, most of the affected people managed to see beyond their pain, overcame their pent-up hatred and disgust, and resolved to work towards a better future together. Former political prisoners shook hands with their erstwhile torturers, and those who had killed civilians for their beliefs, broke down and cried as they embraced the families of their victims and asked for forgiveness. The whole TRC process was full of emotional and inspiring examples of human beings triumphing over their natural desire for revenge, and choosing absolution instead. Today, most of these people are living side-by-side in the new South Africa, free in more ways than one.

Two of the men convicted of the murder of American volunteer worker Amy Biehl today work for the development trust set up in her memory.

One of the most outstanding cases of truth and reconciliation comes from a family who are not South African – the family of the American Fulbright Scholar, Amy Biehl, who was stoned to death in Guguletu, Cape Town, in August 1993. Amy had come to South Africa to help with voter-registration education for the 1994 election, but after dropping some black friends off at their homes, she was killed by youths who had just attended an 'anti-white' political rally. During the TRC proceedings, Amy's parents displayed the most amazing spirit of forgiveness by supporting amnesty for her four killers, they were later released from jail where they were to have served an eighteen-year sentence. Amy's father, Peter, gave up a career in marketing to establish the Amy Biehl Foundation, which raised money in the USA for disadvantaged communities in South Africa. He and his wife Linda, spent their time shuttling back and forth between Los Angeles and Cape Town, and in 1997, the Amy Biehl Foundation Trust was launched in South Africa.

Today the Trust employs 87 South Africans including, remarkably, two of the men convicted of Amy's murder. It runs various projects which employ even more people and benefit thousands of disadvantaged children. One of these projects in the Western Cape makes Amy's Bread and Amy's Milk for sale through major supermarket chains. Profits are donated to the Trust so that it can continue its development work. On the death of Peter Biehl from cancer, his wife said that 'Peter saw great hope in South Africa and also acquired strength from the South African people. He truly believed that it was a miraculous country.' Miraculous indeed. This is one of the many examples that have led other countries with similar histories to look to South Africa as an example of what can be done to put the past behind us and to work towards a better future for all.

Another outcome of the TRC was the Register of Reconciliation, which caused a good deal of controversy and indignation amongst whites when it was first proposed by one of the commissioners, Mary Burton. The Register was established to give ordinary members of the public a chance to express their regret at failing to prevent human-rights violations, and to demonstrate their commitment to reconciliation and a brighter future for South Africa. Mary Burton explains that 'the register has been established in response to a deep wish for reconciliation in the hearts of many South Africans.' A look through some of the entries in the register, available online at www.doj.gov.za/trc/ror/index.htm, brings a lump to one's throat. An Afrikaner from Pretoria wrote simply, 'I am sorry for what I did during the bush war. I am sorry for being a racist during the apartheid years.' Another entry reads, 'I pray that, as the truth about our country's past is being exposed, the Lord will grant us all His wonderful forgiving spirit and His grace to move forward.'

The black gold rush

Moving forward does not simply mean forgetting the past and leaving it behind; it also means righting the wrongs and creating an environment in which the majority of the population can play an active role in the economic success of the country. This is the only way in which those who have suffered will improve their lives. Zimbabwe made the mistake of not doing so sufficiently after independence in 1980, and we are seeing the consequences of that error today. The United States made the same mistake after slaves were freed over a hundred years ago. Black people still comprise the poorest section of their population because the former slaves were never given an adequate hand up to ensure that they could improve their lot.

The South African government is determined not to make the same mistake. They have a policy to promote black economic empowerment, based on recommendations made after two years of research by the Black Economic Empowerment (BEE) Commission, headed by Cyril Ramaphosa. Much criticism is levelled at the concept of black economic empowerment, like the idea that all it is doing is replacing a white business elite with a black business elite, or that efficiencies are decreasing as token black managers are put into positions for which they are ill-prepared. No doubt, there are cases where both of these have happened, but we should look past the fear and unwillingness to change and concentrate on the positive.

There is going to be some degree of short-term pain for a great deal of long-term gain, and the gain is not that far off. The number of black matriculants and graduates has been increasing steadily, according to the South African Institute for Race Relations. Between 1991 and 1998, the number of degrees going to Africans increased by 173 per cent, from 14 798 in 1991 to 40 333 in 1998. And the number is likely to continue to increase. By the time that South Africa has been a true democracy for twenty years, a policy of black economic empowerment may even be unnecessary, because today's generation of black graduates will form the majority of the wealth generators in the country.

'Ex Africa semper aliquid novi.' (Something new always comes out of Africa.)

Pliny the Elder
Roman writer

We can also learn from the example of other countries with a positive outcome to their affirmative action policies, like Malaysia. At the time of independence from Britain 45 years ago, Malaysia was a desperately poor nation. People of Chinese origin, making up a third of the population, effectively controlled the economy, while the indigenous Malaysians, making up over half the population, controlled the government. The Malaysian government put a strict affirmative-action policy into place with the aim of ensuring that the indigenous population controlled at least twenty per cent of the economy within thirty years. In one sense, their economic situation was not that different to ours, and they also experienced problems and resistance implementing the policy. But, over the decade leading up to 1998, the Malaysian economy experienced an eight per cent annual average growth. Today, the world's tallest building is in Kuala Lumpur, and Malaysia has a programme called *Vision 2020* which aims to achieve developed-nation status by

2020. In addition, Malaysians rank themselves among the leading new investors in the South African economy.

No alchemist ever exposed a successful chemical formula without scalding his or her hands at least once. We need to learn from the problems that we have had so far in effecting black economic empowerment, build on our successes, and persist in our goal of creating a more equitable economy.

Service with a smile

The new government took over a country with some severe problems in terms of distribution not only of wealth, but also of access to basic necessities. Lest we forget, South Africa has the second worst distribution of wealth in the world after Brazil. The government's priorities were essentially quite simple, although not at all easy to achieve. They needed to extend the provision of decent housing, education, healthcare and other essential services to the majority of the population, who remained deprived of these basics. Taking into account the task that lay ahead of them, the statistics tell a story of an amazing amount of service delivery in a relatively short space of time.

Over the next three years the government will spend R460 billion on social services, including education, and a further R180 billion on infrastructure.

The South African Advertising Research Foundation, an independent research company, has been measuring standards of living in the country since 1994. SAARF found that between 1994 and 2001, there was a vast improvement in the quality of life for the majority of South Africans. Over this period 1.5 million houses were built, taking the proportion of South Africans who own their own homes up to 77 per cent, compared to 64 per cent in 1994. And, while in 1994 only 58 per cent of houses had electricity and 68 per cent piped water, these percentages had risen to eighty per cent and 76 per cent respectively in 2001.

The equitable distribution of wealth has also improved. The percentage of the population that falls into the category LSM1, the poorest of the poor, fell from twenty per cent in 1994 to five per cent in 2001. At the same time, those earning between R2 500 and R6 000 increased from sixteen per cent to twenty per cent, and those earning over R6 000 increased from ten per cent to eighteen per cent.

And what about education? Literacy levels have increased from 87 per cent to 92 per cent of the population, while the percentage of South Africans who matriculated from secondary school increased from fourteen per cent in 1994 to 23 per cent in 2001. The new curriculum, although controversial, aims to equip students with life skills better than the old system ever did. The whole education system is also in the process of being restructured to ensure more equitable allocation of teachers and resources. Furthermore, the majority of schools have seen a marked improvement in their infrastructures. The 2000 School Register of Needs Survey showed that between 1996 and 2000, the number of schools with no drinking water fell from 34 per cent to 27 per cent, those without electricity fell from 58 per cent to 43 per cent, those with no telephones fell from 61 per cent to 35 per cent and those with no toilets fell from twelve per cent to nine per cent. Over the same period, the number of schools with access to computers and libraries increased and, while the total number of schools rose, the average classroom size (student-to-teacher ratio) dropped.

Granted, there is still a long way to go, but these are encouraging trends over a short period of time. This progress also needs to be read in the context that the government has been economically conservative until now, in order to win the confidence of the international-investment community. As we mention in Chapter 4, now that this has largely been achieved, the government is in a better position to spend more on social improvement than it has done to date.

Saluting social entrepreneurs

South Africa's economic entrepreneurial spirit (discussed in Chapter 5) is not limited to the business arena. There are thousands of ordinary people in civil society who direct their passion, time and skills to tackling some of the country's difficult social challenges, believing that they can and must make a difference.

These are the hands-on alchemists who are helping transform our society at a grassroots level. They are not philanthropists who sit in luxurious homes or offices donating money to charities, and helping people they have never even seen. They are social entrepreneurs who get out there and get their hands dirty. They pursue their social ventures with all the energy, innovation and organisation of private sector businesses, with the notable difference that they often do more with less, their return-on-investment is a better life for their fellow citizens and their dividends are increased hope for the future.

Stars in the Street Universe

One such social entrepreneur is Linzi Thomas who, in 1999, gave up a good career in the film industry to start Street Universe. She believed that someone had to do something concrete to help the homeless children of Cape Town. She was joined six months later by Paddy Upton, who had previously been the physical trainer for the South African cricket team. Using their joint business knowledge and contacts, they built an organisation that seeks to build long-lasting relationships with hardened street kids by offering sporting, recreational and educational alternatives to street life. They also aim to intervene in cases where children have just arrived on the street, seeking to immediately relocate them to a safe 'home' environment.

Street Universe estimates that there are around 450 street kids in Cape Town, and they have identified and gathered information on about 250 of them by getting out onto the street, often at night, and talking to all of them face-to-face. They work closely only with the children who show a real commitment to building a life away from the street and their results have been quite remarkable. National cricketers like Jacques Kallis, Paul Adams, Roger Telemachus and Herschelle Gibbs have worked with the children, and Jacques Kallis has chosen Street Universe as his designated charity. He will sponsor kids who show cricketing potential, allowing them to develop it away from the street. A good example of their success is the story of an eleven-year-old boy who attended the Ryan Maron Cricket School despite having received nine stitches from a stab wound the night before. He was voted by peers as 'best senior fielder'. This opportunity to realise his own potential gave him the courage to phone his mother and ask if he could come home, after two years of life on the street.

Between 1994 and 2000, Eskom connected more than 1 000 households to electricity each day.

Recently, Street Universe received a boost from the international Laureus Sport for Good Foundation. Some of their ambassadors, such as 400-metre hurdles world champion Edwin Moses, decathlete Daley Thompson and rugby heroes Hugo Porta and Morne du Plessis, pledged almost $80 000 to provide sports coaches and development clinics for the kids.

It isn't only on the sports front where the youth are shining. In the first Coca-Cola Popstars TV talent show, eighteen-year-old Frieda Darvel, who sleeps on the pavement outside a shop in Long Street, made it to the Cape Town finals. She sang her way into the top fifty out of nine hundred hopefuls; quite an achievement for someone who lives on the street and has no formal training. It is examples like this that lead those running the organisation to believe that these survivors of street life, who are after all just children, are diamonds in the rough and, if given the chance, will be our future leaders.

Thomas, who started the organisation with nothing but a passionate belief that these children deserve a future, was awarded the Cape Times/V&A Waterfront Woman of Worth award in 2001. The police in Cape Town have also expressed their gratitude for the work Street Universe is doing to uplift the city's street children and keep them away from crime. In a letter to the organisation, they wrote, 'It must be said that the magnanimous work you do without salaries and little help at your disposal can do little else but inspire wonder.'

Angels behind bars

One of the ways in which South Africa is beginning to differentiate itself globally is as a leader in human-rights culture. This is ironic, though not coincidental, given the abysmal track record of human rights abuses during the apartheid era. The human-rights challenge is nowhere more difficult to uphold than in the prison system, where criminals are often scathingly viewed as having forfeited all their rights the moment they chose to commit a crime. It takes a special person to be able to reach beyond this typical 'they deserve what they get' reaction and to see hardened criminals instead as human beings worthy of respect and compassion, no matter how much destruction or pain they have caused. Thankfully, such people *do* exist in South Africa. They are people like Johnny Jansen and Joanna Flanders Thomas, whose story was told in *Fair Lady*'s June 2001 article, 'Where Angels Fear'.

Johnny Jansen took over as head of Pollsmoor Prison's maximum security section in 1997 and was determined to change the culture of brutality that existed there. Jansen's aim was not only to reduce the levels of violence but also to introduce more humane processes in dealing with inmates. He requested that the Centre for Conflict Resolution (CCR) in Cape Town help to implement his vision, and in the few years since the Prison Transformation Programme has been running, there has been a marked drop in violent assaults and gang activity. Attacks have been reduced from about 300 a year in 1997, to approximately twelve a year at present.

Joanna Flanders Thomas, a trainer and facilitator with the CCR, is one of the 'angels' behind this remarkable turnaround at Pollsmoor. She works small miracles on a daily basis with the inmates, most of whom have links to the Cape Flats gangs. Her extraordinary bravery and commitment has seen many prisoners respond successfully and positively to her programme, entitled 'Change is possible, change begins with me.' She holds steadfastly to her belief that 'the only proven method of trying to rehabilitate criminals is to do so with compassion and to treat people as human beings. It doesn't mean we condone what they have done or that we reinforce their bad behaviour,' she is quick to qualify, 'but it goes hand-in-hand with enabling people to take responsibility for themselves, their lives and how their actions affect others.'

Community caretakers

There are some social entrepreneurs in South Africa who inspire us because they do so much with so little. They do not come from privileged backgrounds, nor do they have substantial resources at their disposal. But they see the needs of the community and they respond, in whatever way they can.

Pauline Seroto and Moipone Sekolo are two such national treasures – role models for the power of compassion. They have made it their mission to look after the welfare of destitute children in their dusty township of Kagiso, on the West Rand near Johannesburg. Every day they walk from home to home, checking up on about eighty children living with their grannies, mothers ailing with HIV/AIDS and caregivers, offering various forms of assistance – medical advice (Pauline is an ex-nurse), food and clothing that they have fundraised, help with social-service applications, and good old-fashioned moral support.

Their efforts are under the umbrella of the Sinethemba Community Project, which they started out of a sense of duty as Christians. The project is run from Pauline's living room and the money to fund the work comes largely from their own pockets. Unlike others,

In an effort to relieve the burden on the poor, personal income tax has been cut by almost R50 billion since 1995.

who blame government for its inadequate service delivery, these two remarkable women believe the government is doing its best under adverse circumstances, but that there is a great need for members of the community to rally round and assist.

Their positive attitude in the face of often desperate odds is a lesson to us all. 'This is a poor area and people battle to live, but we do what we can,' says Moipone. 'But for everyone who thinks they are suffering, there is someone down the road who's in a worse situation. Sometimes the work can be heart-breaking and we often sit and cry with frustration.' They say their biggest dream would be to afford a house as a place of safety, where they would be able to protect needy children on a temporary basis until proper care can be arranged. But they are not waiting around for handouts. They continue with their charitable activities irrespective of any support they may, or may not, get.

Another social entrepreneur is Joe Cook, MD of Shep, which takes its name from its mission to help create **S**afe, **H**igh **E**mployment and **P**rosperous communities in

South Africa, through entrepreneur programmes. The organisation's symbol is the hardworking and resolute black and white Border Collie, typically called Shep, that willingly finds and guides sheep into the safety of the kraal.

Examples like these, and others cited in this chapter, are just a few among many thousands that demonstrate how dedicated individuals are steadily transforming South Africa and improving the lives of its people, one at a time. They have realised that the pot of gold at the end of this rainbow nation will only materialise if we each do what we can to make the future brighter. Like Dorothy in the *Wizard of Oz*, they know that getting to that place – 'somewhere over the rainbow' – is a journey; a journey that requires the full engagement of our hearts, our minds and, perhaps most of all, our courage.

It all starts, however, by believing in ourselves, which is what the next chapter is all about.

3 Rekindling the fire within

Talkin' 'bout a revolution

'Smile and the world smiles with you; cry and you cry alone.' We would do well to heed the wisdom of this proverb and apply it to our South African situation. The image we project, as individuals or as a country, shapes others' perceptions of us, and in turn, their confidence in our own potential and prospects for the future. You don't have to be a sports psychologist to know that self-belief is an essential ingredient in achieving success. The same is true off the playing field, in every sphere of life. Why do you suppose companies spend billions on marketing and advertising? They know that building confidence in their brands and creating positive associations with their products is a prerequisite for achieving good sales.

It all comes down to image and, unfortunately for us, there is still a widespread negative image of our country internationally. People generally associate South Africa with its oppressive history, and of course a very limited set of other traits – especially crime, diamonds, gold, wild animals, and being far away from everywhere else – and that's about it.

South Africans abroad do very little to change these perceptions of the country, and in fact many of them go out of their way to entrench the stereotypes of rampant crime, racial discord and an inept government. No doubt, this is one way in which they rationalise the decision they took to leave South Africa in the first place. It is a way to appease any residue of guilty conscience that they may feel for giving up on the country. Marketing academics would call this 'post-sales cognitive dissonance', the process of seeking to confirm that you have made the right buying choice. It really is a great shame, and it certainly doesn't help any of us back in South Africa.

As Peter Hain, born in Nairobi, raised in Pretoria and formerly Britain's Minister for Africa says, 'This country has so much to offer all its citizens. More should trumpet the country's successful transformation from a pariah state to a stable, prosperous democracy respected globally for its progressive constitution, its underlying wealth and natural assets, and the talent of its people. South Africans who travel abroad, whether on business or for employment, need to spread the word and stop whingeing.'

Nelson Mandela is reputed to have said that you aren't doing anyone any favours by being less than you can be – by not achieving your own highest potential. He should know! He has single-handedly done more to re-position perceptions about South Africa around the globe than anyone or anything else. Fortunately, others are starting to follow his powerful example. In fact, we are on the brink of a revolutionary perceptions about our country.

In this chapter, we describe how several initiatives – like National Be Positive Day, Proudly South African and Brand South Africa – are systematically working at re-branding South Africa. These campaigns are using some of the best marketing talents in the world, combined with the lessons of some of the most successful countries and companies, to turn the tide on public perception. Throw in the power of national symbols of pride like the flag and the national anthem and it becomes clear that we are set on a positive path towards the future.

Learning from the Wizards of Oz

Before we contemplate our own navel, though, let's look briefly at how another country, very similar in many ways to our own, has managed to re-brand itself. Before the mid-1980s, Australia didn't feature in the world of 'cool'. At best, it was the brunt of wicked jokes – a society of convicts turned sheep-loving farmers, living in a barren wasteland called the Outback, with a bad case of inbreeding and an accent from hell. It was regarded in much the same way as some people think about Canada – somewhere that everyone knows is out there, but that is too dull or distant to actually find out more about, let alone visit.

All that has changed. Today, Australia is a 'cool' place. Most people know that Nicole Kidman, Russell Crowe, Kylie Minogue and Elle MacPherson are Australians, and these celebrities actually play on the fact because it adds to their appeal. It's hip to be an Aussie. So what happened? Who would have believed that a zany, tongue-in-cheek comedy 'flick' called *Crocodile Dundee*, starring Paul Hogan, would turn it all around? Strange, but true! No matter how unrealistic or skewed a vision of Australia *Crocodile Dundee* gave to foreigners, it put the country on the map and made it tremendously interesting. When this success was followed up by other movies like *Muriel's Wedding*, *Priscilla: Queen of the Desert*, *Strictly*

Ballroom and *Shine*, the world was hooked. People began to flock to Australia on holiday and Fosters beer became a household name in every corner pub of the world. Never mind that Australians themselves hardly drink Fosters – the West was thirsty for something refreshingly different, and Australia was it!

The Australian government had no hesitation in riding on the wave of Aussie fever. Suddenly, there were all sorts of programs in place to punt the country's image – tourism promotion, export incentives, sports development, you name it. Needless to say, their investment paid off handsomely. Having invested heavily in promising young athletes, Australians were very soon winning tournaments and medals in just about every sport out there (they even won gold in speedskating at the 2002 Winter Olympics in Salt Lake City – not bad for a country that's largely desert!). The image-building bonanza culminated in Sydney being awarded the 2000 Summer Olympic Games, which was milked for all it was worth to promote the country even further.

> '**You can't expect investors to have confidence in a country that doesn't have confidence in itself.**'
>
> *FW de Klerk*
> *Former South African president*

Today Australia is still surfing on the crest of its international popularity. Australian soap operas like *Neighbours* and *Home and Away*, broadcast in the UK, tease and tempt the weather-dampened English with flashes of a happy, healthy and sunny lifestyle – not very different, we should add, from the sun-kissed lifestyle that many South Africans enjoy. Australian wines are growing in popularity. Programmes like the American reality-television series, *Survivor*, have taken the Outback into lounges all over the world, and British comedians Billy Connelly and Ben Elton promote the country at every turn (not surprising since both their wives are Australian).

As much as it may irk us, we have to admit that the Australians deserve their success. They have worked hard to make their mark on the world map, not only in the arts, but also in economic terms. They have even beaten us to become the world's largest exporter of proteas. Although proteas are also indigenous to Australia, they are integrally associated with South Africa's identity – the King protea is our national flower. South Africans should be incensed by Australia's dominance and it should be our mission to increase our flower power!

The point is that the Australians have become masters at marketing themselves, and South Africans need to learn a few of their valuable lessons. The building of the Australian brand has gone a long way towards making it easier for Australians to compete. Most importantly, they don't have that perception barrier to overcome. They believe in themselves, they take pride in their unique culture and they are not afraid (even with their funny accent) to shout about it. Soon, we believe, South Africans will be doing the same.

Making Madibaland cool

In South Africa, we may not have Crocodile Dundee, but we do have our own version of an international star – a popular, charming, larger-than-life hero. His name is Nelson Mandela. In the past decade, Mandela has lifted South Africa's international profile immeasurably. For example, when Guy was an exchange student in the USA in 1988, most Americans did not even know that South Africa was a country. Instead there were questions like: 'What country in South Africa do you come from?' and 'Do you live in a hut?' In 2003, a mere fifteen years later, almost everyone knows *something* about South Africa, and it is mostly thanks to our super-cool 'grandfather', Madiba.

'Every day, try to make something out of nothing.'

Outa Lappies
Wandering Karoo recycling artist

Mandela is the symbolic leader of a phenomenon that is sweeping the globe right now, which some are calling 'Chic Afrique', or 'African Cool'. We can't say for sure that Mandela was the catalyst of this new trend, but the fact is that African style is causing quite a stir on the catwalks and in the designer studios of the world. For some years already, African supermodels such as Iman have been considered the ultimate in mystical chic. More recently Diesel, the well-known clothing company and trendsetter, dedicated one of its collections to the concept of 'Le Chic Afreak'. Hermès, French luxury goods retailer, also dedicated one of its recent annual themes to 'The Year of Africa'.

Likewise, images of Africa are creeping into the world of interior design. Many of these take their inspiration from South Africa's game lodges and bush camps that offer the very best of bush décor and design, as Sharna and Daryl Balfour's book entitled *Simply Safari* illustrates. 'The emerging architecture and interiors,' they observe, 'reflect a style of living that is uncomplicated and relaxed, and elemental in its approach to colour, pattern and texture, evoking the character and essence of Africa.' Stephen Falcke's 'Afro chic' makeover of Johannesburg's ultra-luxurious Saxon Hotel is typical of this trend and won him the Interior Designer of the Year Award from Queen Elizabeth II in recognition of his abilities. These trends are important because, as Crocodile Dundee did for Australia, they are helping to reshape the image of our continent and, in turn, popular perceptions of South Africa.

Africa's appeal is growing and we need to grab the opportunity with both hands, like the Australians did in the mid-1980s. Perhaps we should also be looking at the movie business to help put us on the map. What if the next James Bond movie were set in South Africa? Imagine our very own South African Hollywood superstar, Charlize Theron, swooping down from Table Mountain in a paraglider to save Pierce Brosnan's James Bond, as he battles the diamond-smuggling criminal and super-villan, played by Sir Anthony Hopkins. They get blown off course and land in the ocean, and are picked up in a luxury powerboat driven by 007's CIA counterpart, Will Smith. There follows a car chase along a heart-stoppingly precipitous mountain pass in Bond's (made in South Africa) BMW 3-series, nail-biting rock-climbing in the Drakensberg, dune-buggy racing across the Kalahari, a conference with 'M' in a Sandton skyscraper, and finally, Amarula liqueurs at the Waterfront. Fanciful, but you catch the drift, we're sure. If scriptwriters exercised their imaginations and put their Hollywood dream-making machine to work, the possibilities offered by South Africa are endless. We already have a booming film industry in Cape Town, world-class directors like Anant Singh and international best-selling authors like Wilbur Smith. Someone needs to catch the 'Chic Afrique' wave and tell those in Hollywood what we have to offer.

Taking the buffalo by the horns

As entertaining as the above scenario may be, you'll be pleased to know that South Africa is not relying on movie magic or hoping to 'strike it lucky' in order to gain international recognition and spark the perception revolution we so desperately need. Rather, we are taking the buffalo by the horns, through a number of exciting initiatives.

National Be Positive (B+) Day

By 2001, a handful of brave individuals realised that encouraging ex-pats to be positive about South Africa's tourism wonders was not going to be enough on its own. Increasingly, the negative attitudes of South Africans at home were threatening to neutralise all the best efforts of those trying to make a constructive difference. That's when author Stephanie Vermeulen and journalist Sue Grant-Marshall dreamed up the idea of a National Be Positive Day. It was a crazy idea, but they decided to give it a whirl anyway. And, surprise, surprise, the overwhelming response was … well … positive! One of the organisers, Amanda Cunningham, summarised the initiative as 'a call for a ceasefire on whining … before we finally drown in our own bad attitude.'

Most of the media and the public got the point too. On 2 November 2001, our first National Be Positive Day, South Africans had the rare privilege of reading positive news. (The journalists must have had to work much harder that day, since negative news is always easier to find and report on, no matter which country you're in.) Suddenly there were articles acknowledging that our government was delivering remarkable results in economic policy, international trade, provision of basic services, and yes, even in tackling crime. There were also numerous stories of courageous individuals who are making a real difference to the lives of fellow South Africans, energised by their commitment to the upliftment of the country. These were not achievements or people that had suddenly appeared overnight but, for once, they were being recognised in our national media.

> **'To be positive means to enjoy the rare gift of hope. It means confidence that tomorrow will be better than today ... Our country has great need of such people.'**
>
> *Thabo Mbeki*
> *President of South Africa*

In an article entitled 'South Africans have reason to be positive', President Mbeki said: 'I commend this Day and what it seeks to achieve for all our people. To be positive means to enjoy the rare gift of hope. It means confidence that tomorrow will be better than today. It indicates the possibility of seeing further than one's nose and therefore further than today's problems, and thus seeing into the promise of the future. It signifies the commitment of the positive person to contribute to making tomorrow a better day both for himself or herself and for all our communities. Our country has great need of such people.'

Proudly South African

Around the same time as the first National Be Positive Day, the Proudly South African campaign was launched as a concrete outcome of the 1998 Presidential Jobs Summit, where the idea was first mooted. Bringing the idea to fruition was the responsibility of the National Economic Development and Labour Council (Nedlac), supported by organised business, labour, government and the community.

The campaign aims to promote those South African companies, products and services which are helping substantially to build our economy, and which are socially responsible. The eye-catching Proudly South African logo gives consumers who want to support the campaign a way to identify these companies and products. Companies who wish to use the logo must meet the following criteria: local content (at least fifty per cent of the cost of production must be retained in South Africa); quality (the company or product must meet high-quality standards); commitment to fair labour standards; and sound environmental practices. In addition to being allowed to associate the logo with their products or services, member companies also enjoy the benefit of a R30-million media campaign, that has been earmarked to promote the Proudly South African brand.

Kevin Wakeford, former CEO of the SA Chamber of Business, summed up the basic concept of the campaign as follows: 'By combining a badge of origin with a quality endorsement, we can give companies a competitive edge

Every R1 million spent on local products creates between five and thirty jobs.

here and overseas.' The campaign also has the backing of other heavyweights. President Mbeki sees the campaign as 'vital for our economic growth'. Willie Madisha, President of national labour union, Cosatu, wants workers 'not only to be proud South Africans, but also to play a leading role in this campaign.' Khulu Mbongo, Secretary General of the SA Youth Council, believes Proudly South African will be 'helping to shape young people's purchasing patterns in the years to come.'

The concept behind Proudly South African was neither new nor unique, having been successfully implemented in other forms in other countries such as Australia, India, Italy, Malaysia, New Zealand, Thailand and the USA. In Australia, for example, 95 per cent of consumers recognise the 'Australian Made' campaign brand and 92 per cent say it influences their buying decisions. Products carrying the campaign logo now represent the equivalent of over R25 billion.

Despite the precedent set by these other countries, Nedlac did their homework before launching the Proudly South African campaign. Specially-commissioned research showed that 92 per cent of South Africans believe that South Africa needs a campaign to promote consumers and companies sourcing their goods locally. The research showed further that 77 per cent of people already make some effort to seek out South African goods on the shelf. Of all the criteria that would encourage them to buy a locally-made product, good quality and contributing to the economic upliftment of the country were the most motivating. Research by the University of Cape Town also indicated that for every R1 million spent on local products instead of imports, a minimum of between five and thirty jobs will be created, depending on the industry.

So the results showed that the campaign should go ahead. The next step was to recruit Martin Feinstein, a dynamic force in media and marketing, to run the campaign, as well as to secure the overarching support of radio and television presenter, Tim Modise, as chairman. 'Now every South African can be a nation-builder,' says Modise. 'As South Africans, we often forget how innovative, entrepreneurial and competitive we can be. We need to find a new sense of pride in who we are and what we can achieve. With the Proudly South African campaign, companies can identify themselves as such for everyone to see.'

By November 2002, a year after being launched, Proudly South African had more than 450 members, including founding sponsors Old Mutual, Eskom, South African Airways, Barloworld and Telkom. Why not support Proudly South African companies and let your money make a difference?

Brand South Africa

In 2001, Yvonne Johnston was 'called up for duty' by the President's office. She was recognised as a talented strategic marketer who had held directorships in some of South Africa's most influential ad agencies. She'd been voted the country's top media director, chaired the Media Directors Circle, and had been a judge for all the country's top press awards. Little did she know that a mind-blowing challenge and opportunity was about to be offered to her – to become CEO of the International Marketing Council of South Africa (IMC). The IMC is charged with branding the country as the most attractive nation in the world.

Niall FitzGerald, global chairman of Unilever, a company recognised as a leader in fast-moving consumer goods, *gave* his company's strategic brand-marketing model to President Mbeki to help the IMC develop South Africa as a brand. FitzGerald, who lived in South Africa for a period earlier in his career, has a strong belief in the future of South Africa, and he further displayed his commitment by seconding one of his expert marketers to the IMC. Led by this world-class branding team, extensive market research was commissioned to find out what people's hopes and fears for South Africa really are. This included a thousand interviews with South Africans at all levels of society and hundreds more with local and international business executives and tourists. A number of positive themes emerged, around which South Africa's national brand will be built. They are:

- *Forging the better way*

  South Africa has forged ahead, facing obstacles, challenges and adversity along the way. Through it all, South Africa has continued to press on because it is a land rich in its people and rich in its resources. So South Africa has come to make its own path – a new and better way, built of courage, determination and innovation. A path to the future for all.

- *People success*

  The smaller the world becomes, the further apart people grow. Well, not everywhere. Not in South Africa ... because South Africa is a land of ordinary people doing extraordinary things. Because South Africans share a passion; a determination; a vision and, above all, a soul. It is this collective humanity (*ubuntu*) that makes South Africa bigger than its borders.

- *Active adaptability*

  'Change is the only constant.' Success depends on how you respond to it. South Africa is a country of change; changing landscapes and changing economies. South Africans are a nation born of change, a nation that can rise to the challenge of change, that welcomes it, and not only adapts to it, but embraces it wholeheartedly. We use the learning from our journey to enable us to make quantum leaps, thus flourishing in a changing world.

Brand South Africa's approach to promoting our country is consistent with the way in which successful global companies like Unilever build a brand for their products. For example, they have defined our competitive environment (all emerging countries), target market (anyone who can have a positive effect on the lives of South Africans), key discriminators (South Africa's ability to inspire the world to a new way of doing things, because our unique combinations create refreshing possibilities) and South Africa's brand essence ('Alive with possibility!').

Having had South Africa's desired brand identity agreed right up to Presidential level, a massive communication strategy has now kicked in. The objective of this media campaign is to transform the image of South Africa internally and externally by inspiring a mindset of confidence in South Africa, and by creating a single-minded and tailored South African brand. The vision is that, in a few years' time, the image of South Africa that is projected to the world will be a positive one, comprising a consistent message that all South Africans and friends of South Africa believe in and are passionately energised by. Yvonne Johnston's conclusion is unequivocal – 'South Africa is going to become invincible.' We agree.

The Homecoming Revolution

The creative talent of independent advertising agency morrisjones&co also agrees. So much so that they are putting their professional branding expertise into a voluntary initiative that they have called 'The Homecoming Revolution'. The primary objective is to persuade ex-patriate South Africans to come home. An advertising campaign is being developed to roll out in the United Kingdom, Canada, Australia, New Zealand and the USA.

Figures from government data agency Statistics SA show that, in the first nine months of 2002, close to 9 000 South Africans emigrated. Workers are being lost in important fields such as teaching, nursing, engineering, accounting and IT. 'The brain drain is costing South Africa R2.5 billion each year and it's time we did something about it,' says Angel Jones, Creative Director of morrisjones&co and founder of The Homecoming Revolution. 'The exodus is not increasing, thank goodness. It's now levelling out and the time is ripe to reverse it.'

'This country engages all the senses, and even the soul.'

Moeketsi Mosola
Chief Operating Officer
South African Tourism

morrisjones&co conducted some dipstick research in which an overwhelming 78 per cent of respondents said that they did not intend to leave South Africa permanently. However, they did say that they would perceive themselves as failures if they returned home without 'achieving something' overseas.

For morrisjones&co, this was an exciting discovery because of the way that advertising can change perceptions. The driving message of The Home-coming Revolution is: 'Don't wait until it gets better – come home and make it better'.

The first part of the campaign will encourage ex-pats to refer to our country as 'home' instead of just 'South Africa'. The Homecoming Revolution won't position South Africa as the 'poor cousin' at the bottom of the African continent and in dire need of help. Instead it will brand the country as a trendy, happening, developing nation. The place where it's *AT*. (A selection of the launch ads can be found at the end of this book.)

The second part of the campaign will profile ex-pats who have returned and will run in more mainstream international media. The testimonials are living-eating-breathing *reasons to believe*. The returnees will share their stories and reveal how, although it's not been all plain sailing, they made the right decision to come home.

The ads acknowledge the continuing problems of crime and AIDS. Positive themes focus on the entrepreneurial opportunities, the rush of diversity, the great lifestyle and the chance to really make a difference. 'We will ensure that we don't paint an unrealistic bowl-of-cherries scenario,' says Jones. 'We acknowledge that it is a trade off to come back, so the communication will be very realistic.'

The encouraging news, according to Jones, is that people are indeed starting to come back. Corporate head-hunters and estate agents say they have seen a noticeable increase in the number of returning executives in 2001 and 2002. They're mostly highly-skilled entrepreneurs who are making their own opportunities. Some returnees have started their own businesses, some are carving out a family-life, some are climbing up the corporate ladder and some are working at grassroots level and are sharing their skills with others. This is what some returnees think about coming home:

'The developments in Gauteng are astounding, and pregnant with opportunity for those willing to get stuck in … an open-minded and experimental culture has made it easier to operate as an independent.' – Kimon Phitidis, Communications Consultant

'Because of the high levels of competition in London, it would have taken us years to get to the same position that we reached in a matter of months in South Africa.' – Clare McKenzie, Promotions Director

'I'm loving Jo'burg. My dearest friends are all here and, as part of a young couple starting out on their lives together, it is cool to be in a happening city.' – John Reardon, Banker

'There are great business opportunities here. It's not a saturated market like the USA, EU or Asia. Sure, there are problems, but on the whole, this is the best place to be.' – Nina Pearse, IT specialist

'I gained an enormous amount of experience abroad and I plan to start my own architectural firm at home. I believe that this country offers a dynamic environment for young people with passion and a vision for the future.' – Tina Gallagher, Architect

'I woke up one morning, during a brief visit home, saw sunlight spill like liquid syrup through a gap in the curtains, and realised I hadn't felt that happy in a long time.' – Lucinda Hooley, Actress

United we shall stand

Beyond these specific campaigns, there are also various powerful symbols of our unity as a nation, which help us to connect wholeheartedly with everything our country stands for. These symbols, like our flag and anthem, give us a common focal point through which to channel our pride and express our joy at being South African. Even the stories of their origin are a source of fascination and inspiration.

Pinning our colours to the mast

The South African flag is reportedly the third most recognisable flag in the world, embraced by newly-proud South Africans and firmly woven into the psyche of the rainbow nation – a lively symbol of unity, of nation-building in a vibrant, diverse land in which anything is possible. Few people know that the new flag nearly didn't see the light of day, just at the time when we needed it most, when our new nation was being born. The story of our flag is told in the colourful book, *Flying with Pride*, by Denis Beckett.

Selecting a new national flag was part of the negotiation process towards the new dispensation which was set in motion when Nelson Mandela was released from prison in 1990. In order to find a design that was nationally representative, a nationwide competition for public proposals was launched in 1993. More than 7 000 designs were received. Based on the submissions, six designs were drawn up by the National Symbols Commission and presented to the public and the Negotiating Council – but none of them elicited enthusiastic support.

As a result, a number of design studios were contracted to submit further proposals – again without the desired result. Parliament went into recess at the end of 1993 without a suitable design for the new flag. In mid-February, chief party political negotiators, Cyril Ramaphosa and Roelf Meyer, were tasked with resolving the flag issue. A final design was adopted on 15 March 1994 – derived from a design developed by the State Herald (Fred Brownell). The proclamation of the new national flag was published on 20 April 1994 – only seven days before the new flag was to be inaugurated on the 27th. This created an enormous challenge for flag manufacturers, but the task was accomplished in time.

Since that day, this bright national symbol that so easily lends itself to being a fashion statement, has taken on myriad shapes and forms and virtually any application you can think of – from funky clothing and accessories, to cushion covers and cigarette lighters. South African Airways' aircraft, with their attractive tail design, literally blaze our flag across the world's skies. And nowhere is the flag more visible than in sports stadiums around the world, whenever a South African team is playing. Even the remotest locations seem to bring flag-waving South Africans out of the closet. And, let's be honest, when we see our victorious sports stars donning a brightly coloured flag cape, like the supermen and superwomen that they are, our hearts swell with pride.

Cheryl Carolus, CEO of South African Tourism and former South African High Commissioner to the United Kingdom, believes the high visibility of the South

African flag is a sign that 'South Africans don't skulk around hiding who they are. You see our flags everywhere, even at the military tattoo in Scotland and at the London Marathon. South Africans travel with their flag and take it out at any occasion.'

From an image-marketing perspective we could not ask for a more distinctive and recognisable symbol with which to paint South Africa boldly across the canvas of the global mindscape. Like the Americans and the Brits, our flag is set to become one of our most prized possessions, representing everything that we love and cherish about the place and promise of South Africa. Importantly, our flag incorporates the colours of virtually every other country on the African continent too – so it is also a symbol of the African Renaissance. Let's get behind our flag and wave it wildly at the rest of the world! Check out www.saflag.com for inspiration.

Singing with soul

Nkosi Sikelel' iAfrika ('God Bless Africa') is a song of solidarity sung throughout Africa and forms the first half of South Africa's official national anthem. The original version was composed as a isiXhosa hymn in 1897 by Enoch Sontonga, a teacher at a Methodist mission school in Johannesburg. Most of Sontonga's songs were sad, bearing witness to the suffering of African people, but their inspiring lyrics and haunting melodies were popular and after his death in 1905, choirs used to borrow his music from his wife.

Solomon Plaatje, one of South Africa's greatest writers and a founding member of the ANC, was the first to have Nkosi Sikelel' iAfrika recorded in London in 1923. In 1927, seven additional isiXhosa stanzas were added by poet Samuel Mqhayi and a Sesotho version was published almost two decades later, in 1942, by Moses Mphahlele. Even to this day, there are no standard versions or translations of the original, so words vary from place to place and from occasion to occasion. Generally, the first stanza is sung in Xhosa or Zulu, followed by the Sesotho version.

It was the Rev JL Dube's Ohlange Zulu Choir which popularised Nkosi Sikelel' iAfrika at concerts in Johannesburg and it became a favourite church hymn as well as a rallying cry at political meetings. As the struggle for freedom intensified, Nkosi Sikelel' iAfrika became regarded as South Africa's unofficial national anthem and it was always sung as an act of defiance against the apartheid regime, not only in South Africa, but around the world.

When liberation finally dawned in 1994, newly-elected President, Nelson Mandela, proclaimed the old national anthem ('Die Stem') and Nkosi Sikelel' iAfrika as dual anthems. In 1996, a shortened, combined version of the two anthems was released, carrying the title, Nkosi Sikelel' iAfrika. Today, this remarkable anthem regularly produces a tear in the eye when it is sung with varying levels of gusto, but always with undeniable national pride.

Nkosi Sikelel' iAfrika is such a beautiful and uplifting hymn, which so poignantly expresses the hopes and prayers of millions of people on this continent and around the world, that we include the lyrics of the classic version (Original Lovedale English Translation) below, thus ending this chapter on a high note!

God Bless Africa

Lord, bless Africa
May her horn rise up high
Hear Thou our prayers
And bless us.

Descend, O Spirit
Descend, O Holy Spirit.

Bless our chiefs
May they remember their Creator
Fear Him and revere Him
That He may bless them.

Bless the public men
Bless also the youth
That they may carry the land with patience
And that Thou mayst bless them.

Bless the wives
And also all the young women
Lift up all the young girls
And bless them.

Bless the ministers
Of all the churches of this land
Imbue them with Thy Spirit
And bless them.

Bless agriculture and stockraising
Banish all famine and disease
Fill the land with good health
And bless it.

Bless our efforts
Of union and self-upliftment
Of education and mutual understanding
And bless them.

Lord, bless Africa
Blot out all its wickedness
And its transgressions and sins
And bless it.

Amen!

4 Launchpad for prosperity

One of the favourite dinner-talk topics in South Africa is our supposedly flailing economy. And yet the South African economy has been expanding while the rest of the world has been faltering and struggling to come out of recession. While South Africans celebrated a GDP growth of around three per cent in 2002, some economies, like Japan, have actually been shrinking. In fact, according to Iraj Abedian, Chief Economist at Standard Bank, South Africa is within the top-seven best-performing economies in the world.

This can be attributed to a number of developments, including the weakness of the rand exchange rate that we mentioned earlier in this book. More than any one factor, however, it is a positive sign of the solid foundations that have been built upon by the country's economic aficionados over the past several years. In this chapter, we take a closer look at those foundations and investigate some of the economy's growth superstars. Out of necessity, this chapter maintains a relatively broad view. Things change so rapidly that, while we are writing that the world is in recession today, it may be that it will be well on its way towards recovery by the time that you read this.

Laying solid foundations

Most governments that take over from an incumbent seek to change the status quo, especially in the developing world. This is not only their prerogative, but it is usually expected by the electorate which voted for reform in the first place. Besides which, politicians feel that they have a limited amount of time in which to make their mark, so that they can be voted in again, next time around. This happens to an even more radical degree when the take-over is revolutionary, or when the new regime's policies are fundamentally different to those of their predecessors. Often there follows some form of mass nationalisation (as with many

African countries in the 1960s and '70s) or conversely mass privatisation (such as under Margaret Thatcher's rule in 1980s Britain).

Perhaps that is why everyone expected the new South African government under the ANC, which had long been aligned to the SA Communist Party (SACP) and Cosatu, to nationalise the mines, the banks and pretty much everything else, and using their revenues to spend like mad on inefficient employment-creation projects. Many are still convinced, despite the facts, that this will happen, as they wait like prophets of doom for the government to make its move to seize farms, attach mines or generally do what they believe it is predisposed to do.

What this outlook ignores is several key facts in our favour. Firstly, we have a large number of highly-educated people in power. Many, if not most, have studied, lived or worked overseas. Those that have returned from exile, like President Mbeki, have lived and studied in Western Europe, the USA, Eastern Europe and Africa. They have thus been able to learn, from first-hand experience, of the failures and successes of the policies in those countries. In addition, Mbeki has made some prudent appointments in the areas of trade and finance, in particular the so-called 'finance quartet' of Alec Erwin (Minister of Trade & Industry), Trevor Manuel (Minister of Finance), Maria Ramos (Director General of the Treasury) and Tito Mboweni (Governor of the Reserve Bank). These leaders have also been supported by highly-experienced professionals in their departments, who continued to serve their ministries after the change of government in 1994.

Tightening the purse strings

Perhaps the ANC government managed to exercise fiscal restraint, despite criticism from the poorer sections of the population which expected more improvement faster, because it has not had to worry that it is in real danger of losing the next election. And while it is certainly not desirable for a government to lack an effective opposition, we are fortunate the current government has used this breathing space wisely to lay the groundwork for long-term growth by ensuring that social spending takes place responsibly.

The 'finance quartet's' focus has been on following a prudent macroeconomic strategy in order to ensure that the rest of the world develops faith in our economy, as being stable and positioned for growth. Once this has been achieved, South Africa can consider increasing public spending for employment creation and other poverty-alleviation programmes.

On the monetary-policy side, the Treasury has set an ambitious target range for inflation for the next few years – three to six per cent until 2003 and three to five per cent in 2004/2005. Although prior to November 2001 it looked very much like we would meet the targets, we did not make it in 2002 and possibly will not in 2003. The reasons for this are unfortunately somewhat beyond our control – the price of oil increased dramatically after the 9/11 attacks in the USA, and the dollar strengthened markedly against the rand. These factors influenced prices here at home.

What we should be focussing on though, is the fact that we are in a position to set such a target range in the first place. We very easily forget that for twenty years or more South Africa had double-digit inflation, and a range of three to six per cent was unthinkable. Also significant is that Tito Mboweni, the man responsible for ensuring that the inflation targets are met, stuck to his guns and raised interest rates numerous times during 2002 in order to beat inflation back down. This consistency, despite upsetting consumers, has won him widespread respect from economists.

According to *The Economist's* annual Big Mac index, South Africa has the cheapest Big Mac hamburger in the world.

It isn't easy managing an economy though, because increasing interest rates has the possible effect of dampening economic growth. It's a delicate balance; something that Trevor Manuel really wants to get right. He too has won admiration for doing what he says he will do, like when he promised in 2001 that there would be tax cuts for lower- and middle-income groups in 2002, and there were. These cuts, along with other fiscal-policy measures such as better tax collection and improved government spending, are amongst Manuel's economic tools which he hopes will help to lift growth to 3.7 per cent by 2004. This prudence will put us in a far better position to alleviate poverty in the long term, and thus reduce the massive differences in income from which so many of our other problems stem.

Weaving more egg baskets

The structure of the South African economy has changed dramatically over the past few decades. Many people wistfully refer back to the days when one rand bought more than one dollar, and it was 'so cheap' to travel to the USA. The point that they miss is that the rand was strong only because of the incredibly-high gold price. In the early 1980s, gold fetched over $800 an ounce and South Africa produced over seventy per cent of the Western World's gold. Today gold is considered to be doing very well at around $300 an ounce. Unfortunately, the revenues of those heady days did not help to change the economy structurally, and we continued to be almost entirely reliant on the export of primary goods, such as agricultural products and mineral ores, as opposed to valued-added goods like furniture and motor cars.

Today, we no longer put all our economic eggs in one basket. Only thirty per cent of total exports are unrefined primary goods, and the share of gold exports as a percentage of total exports fell from 22 per cent in 1996 to 14 per cent in 2000. Over the same period, annual export growth of manufactured goods increased from twenty per cent to 24 per cent. Our export markets are also far more diversified, even when compared with other leading economies around the world. While Europe is still our biggest trading partner, we are not reliant on only one or two countries or regions for our export earnings.

Prior to the '80s, we were also very dependent on imports and foreign-owned companies for most of our manufactured goods. That changed during the period of sanctions and disinvestment, when foreign governments forced their companies to stop supplying South Africa with imports and to shed their South African subsidiaries. Perversely, this actually did our economy some good in the long run, as companies like Barclays (now First National Bank) and Mobil (now Engen) were sold to local buyers, leading to a higher percentage of local ownership of already-strong companies. Although the period of apartheid isolation led to a lot of necessary but painful restructuring during our eventual reintegration into the world economy, it does mean that we now have more control over our own destiny and it helps to shield us to some degree from the ups and downs of international markets.

Locally-owned companies are often more adventurous than their former foreign owners, investing increasingly in the promising African market. South Africa, for example, is the biggest foreign investor in Mozambique, with some 250 companies present there. This is particularly true in the financial-services sector. Our banks are the most powerful in Africa and are increasingly comparable to many of the larger banks elsewhere in the world. In fact, financial-services companies like Old Mutual and Investec are expanding around the globe, and the JSE Securities Exchange is rapidly forging alliances with exchanges in other countries – a sign of its strength and international standing.

Laying down new tracks

Despite all the shortcomings of the old-South African economy, there was at the very least significant development of the country's 'First World' infrastructure. The extensive transportation, energy and communications networks have not been neglected since the change of government, but rather used as a platform for further development.

We have seven good deep-water ports, which are busier than ever and increasingly so, and plans are underway to build another one at Coega in the Eastern Cape. Coega, which is estimated to be the largest single long-term investment in our history, is expected to create 10 000 jobs directly by way of multi-billion-rand investments in the construction of the port, a stainless steel works and an envisaged aluminium smelter, among other possible business ventures.

We have 34 000 km of railway line to get goods from those ports to pretty much anywhere else in the country and vice versa. This rail network also connects into the networks of other African countries, enabling us to move products throughout the continent. In addition, we have over 6 000 km of tarred highways and main roads to cover the rest of the country.

Johannesburg International Airport won the 'African Airport of the Year Award', at the Annual World Travel Awards, three years in a row (1999 to 2001).

Transport Minister, Dullah Omar, as the person ultimately responsible for this network, recognises that 'there is clearly room for improvement and we need to make it more efficient', and that is what he is working towards.

Already the existing airports are being put through massive upgrades by the Airports Company of South Africa, which is planning for a substantial increase in the movement of both people and cargo over the next ten years.

In South Africa, we can use our existing infrastructure to grow the country from a good economy into a great one.

Making the right connection

Our existing communications and IT infrastructure is being expanded to develop a competitive advantage for South Africa. A new 'Jo'burg 2030' initiative has been launched with the aim of setting the city up as the IT and service-oriented hub of Africa. For any global player wanting a piece of the African pie, Johannesburg will be the entry point. The Gauteng government has also started the Blue IQ project, aiming to spend R3.5 billion over the next three years to set up the infrastructure required by modern knowledge-based sectors. It expects to generate R100 billion and 100 000 new jobs for the province over the next fifteen to twenty years. At the same time, Cape Town is vying to do the same and better. The Cape IT Initiative (CITI) aims to make Cape Town the IT-development hub of choice for organisations around the world – a Southern Hemisphere Silicon Valley. Through one of its recently-launched projects, The Cape Lab, it is helping technology entrepreneurs break into the global market.

The importance of the hi-tech sector is not lost on our national government, which has been seeking the guidance of global IT masters who serve on the President's International Advisory Council on Information, Society and Development. These include Larry Ellison (CEO of Oracle), Carly Fiorina (CEO of HP), Reza Mahdavi (CEO of Cisco), local whizz-kid Mark Shuttleworth and others. The council aims to ensure that South Africa uses technology to develop and transform itself, and become increasingly competitive internationally.

The government has also committed to selling a large stake in the telecommunications parastatal, Telkom, and introducing a second fixed-line operator soon. The privatisation and opening up of the market will help to make our communications infrastructure even more advanced. South Africa already has the highest number of internet users in Africa, at 2.5 million currently, and we are leading the way in the mobile phone industry on the continent with some seven million subscribers. South African companies are taking the experience gained here and spreading it around Africa with, for example, investments by MTN in Nigeria and Vodacom in Tanzania. The opportunities are huge. The UN's International Telecommunication Union recently reported that the number of cell-phone users in Africa has vaulted up from two million in 1997 to thirty million in 2001, and that number is growing fast.

It isn't only in the high-tech areas where we are benefiting from our existing infrastructure. Eskom, which generates around 200 000 GWh of the world's cheapest electricity, is bringing electricity to millions of South Africans, while also investing in significant projects throughout the rest of Africa. Eskom already generates seventy per cent of Africa's electricity, and it is leading a campaign to light up the continent with a continent-wide grid by 2010, possibly exporting surplus electricity to Europe and the Middle East.

The Johannesburg Stock Exchange (JSE) is the fifteenth-largest stock exchange in the world.

Awakening the sleeping giant

What's the big deal?

In our rapidly-globalising yet inequitable world, developed countries are feeling increasingly pressured to help developing countries improve by offering them preferential trade agreements. An example of this is the Africa Growth and

Opportunities Act (AGOA) in the United States, which provides a number of African countries with the opportunity to export certain products with a significant reduction in import duties. Of all the African states eligible for AGOA, South Africa is best positioned to take advantage of this benefit because of our more-developed industries and sophisticated infrastructure. To illustrate this, in the period September 2001 to September 2002, over half of our exports to the US qualified for duty-free provisions of AGOA compared with only 8.1 per cent for the rest of the AGOA countries. Indeed South African exports to the US under AGOA almost doubled in the same period. Some industries, like the automotive industry, have seen major benefits from AGOA. BMW now produces its 3-series cars destined for America in South Africa rather than in Germany, in order to take advantage of the lower tariffs on cars made in South Africa.

The European Union has also opted to work out an agreement with South Africa, as part of its drive to support developing nations. This trade, development and cooperation agreement removes barriers on ninety per cent of all trade between South Africa and the countries of the EU. The benefits are obvious when one considers how much cheaper our products are than goods of the same quality built in Europe. Not surprisingly, exports have already grown as a direct result.

An analysis by the Clothing Federation of South Africa suggests the improved export opportunities offered under AGOA could lift clothing sector employment by 74 per cent within five years.

Closer to home, our government is committed to developing a free-trade area between the fourteen member countries of the Southern African Development Community, which will further assist the growth of exports to our neighbours. South Africa is also in talks with the countries of Mercosur (the group of countries in the South American free-trade association), China, Australia and various others, about preferential trade agreements. In another development it is hoped that Russia will re-classify South Africa as a developing country. This is significant because until now we have been classified as 'developed', and the change in status will allow our products to attract significantly less in import duties.

It seems that now, in stark contrast to the way things were, everyone wants to deal with us. Well, why should we complain? It's great not being a pariah state!

Kickstarting the African Renaissance

Despite widespread perceptions to the contrary, the face of African politics has changed dramatically for the better since the end of the Cold War, as a few figures can demonstrate. From 1985 to 1989, only nine sub-Saharan countries held 'competitive' (free and fair) elections. In the five years that followed, that number more than quadrupled to 38. The average share of legislative seats won by opposition parties rose from ten per cent in 1989 to 31 per cent in 1994. Of these 38 elections, 29 were founding elections that broke the monopoly on politics held by authoritarian regimes.

The 1990s also saw the rise of a new generation of African leaders. Before 1990, more than nine out of ten incoming national leaders were appointed by military or party elites. However, between 1990 and 1994, democratic leadership transitions took place in eleven countries.

South Africa has been part of this sea change on the continent. Now we're playing an important role in keeping the momentum going – lending our diplomatic skills to peace-brokering efforts in numerous regions in Africa, and encouraging the spread of democracy among its nations. Most recently, this has been visible in Mbeki's leadership role in the creation of the African Union and NEPAD.

Four of South Africa's banks rank among the world's top 500.

In 2002, the Organisation of African Unity (OAU) was reborn as the African Union (AU). This is more than just a name change as it represents a significant change in sentiment on the continent. While the OAU defined itself in terms of what it stood against (colonialism, racism and Cold War-era foreign interference), the new legal framework of the AU defines it by what it stands for (democracy, good governance and respect for human rights). The AU's structure and responsibilities are now in line with international legal trends, and it is loosely modelled along the lines of the European Union and the UN.

It is Africa's new leaders, including South Africa's President Mbeki, Nigeria's President Obasanjo and Senegal's President Wade, who have begun taking responsibility for Africa's economic recovery through initiatives like NEPAD (New Partnership for Africa's Development).

Officially, NEPAD is the AU's economic and development plan. In a broader sense, it is a strategy to make Africa's renaissance happen, similar to the Marshall Plan that helped to rejuvenate Europe and Japan after the Second World War.

Mbeki's idea is of a rebirth that rids the world of Afro-pessimism, develops the African economy and instils peace, security and democracy. NEPAD's codes of conduct will commit each member state to multiparty democracy, sensible economic and financial policies, the sanctity of private property and the rule of law.

Rejuvenation will be achieved on three levels. Firstly, NEPAD will negotiate on behalf of member countries for things such as better trade access and debt relief. Secondly, practical programmes will ensure that pressing social problems such as health and education are addressed. Thirdly, NEPAD will set standards for good governance and implement a peer-review system designed to put pressure on undemocratic states to change their ways. A committee will assess compliance with these standards every three years.

In the year to the end of August 2002, foreigners were net buyers of R6.147-bn worth of South African bonds.

It may seem like the AU and NEPAD have some lofty goals, and certainly there are many sceptics who will wait to see positive changes before believing in them, but what they are doing is setting an agenda which has the potential to change negative sentiment about Africa and prepare the ground for a sustained economic boom on the continent. South Africa, as a key regional player, stands to gain enormously in the process. NEPAD needs our active support, not our passive criticism.

Nothing succeeds like success

Some of this good news and economic potential seems finally to be filtering through. International agencies, like Moody's and Standard & Poors, which produce economic ratings that are widely used as a measure of a country's investment attractiveness, have consistently been offering votes of confidence in South Africa's economic future by upgrading our ratings. Positive spin-offs include the fact that during the first seven months of 2002, foreigners bought a net R6.147 billion of South African bonds. When the treasury issued South Africa's biggest bond ever in April 2002 – $1 billion with a ten-year maturity and the lowest-ever coupon for a dollar-denominated bond of 7.375 per cent – it attracted orders of more than $2 billion from 120 international investors. This demand, along with the fact that Standard & Poors assigned a favourable BBB-minus debt rating to the bond, was seen as a clear signal of confidence by foreign investors in South Africa's solid economic fundamentals and consistent economic policies.

Locally, too, business confidence hit an eight-year high in the second quarter of 2002, despite the prospect of missing the inflation target, despite the low rand, and despite problems faced by economies in the rest of the world. It reached 68 points, when measured by the independent Bureau for Economic Research. This tops the previous high of 67 points in the fourth quarter of 1994, when the euphoria of the peaceful transition to democracy was at its peak.

While we still have a way to go in changing the negative perceptions that exist about South Africa, especially abroad, these are positive signs that the road ahead might just be smoother than it has been over the past few decades and that we could be in for some good growth in the future. The more confidence foreigners and locals have in our economy, the more likely they will be to invest and contribute to economic development.

Leaders of the pack

As we mentioned earlier, South African exports are already doing well. South Africa currently has the third-highest export growth rate in the world. In the 44 months up to July 2002, there was a trade surplus in 39 of those months, which basically means that we sold

The Mercedes Benz C Class, BMW 3-Series and VW Golf and Jetta vehicles, for all right-hand drive markets in the world, are produced in South Africa.

more to foreigners than we bought from them. Certain specific examples stand out, such as the fact that in 1994 trade with Nigeria was worth $12 million, and this had grown to $400 million by 2001. There are also some shining stars amongst exporting industries that are beating records and experiencing unprecedented growth; these we'd like to highlight now.

Motoring ahead

Probably the most notable of South Africa's export-growth areas is the motor industry. This industry, which during the 1980s was inefficient, uncompetitive, over-protected and beset by industrial unrest, has proved to be an example of how business and government can work together to develop a world-class industry.

A good deal of the industry's success has been attributed to the Motor Industry Development Plan (MIDP), introduced in 1995, which allows manufacturers to offset import duties with export credits. The MIDP has encouraged motor manufacturers to concentrate on producing only a few models of vehicles locally for export, and to import other models. In this way, they have been able to increase their production runs of certain models, thus reducing unit costs, increasing productivity and improving competitiveness. When it was first introduced, the industry predicted that it would not be able to compete internationally and that there would be thousands of jobs lost: In fact, the opposite has happened, with billions being invested in undertaking rapid structural change to the industry in a relatively short period of time, and exports increasing beyond the wildest expectations. The current MIDP is due to end in 2007, but Trade Minister Alec Erwin has indicated that it will continue with a few amendments to further increase competitiveness.

The results of the program speak for themselves. In 1995 the automotive industry generated R4.2 billion in exports, just 4.1 per cent of South Africa's total exports. In 2001 automotive exports reached R30 billion, twelve per cent of total exports. The industry expects this amount to increase to R75 billion by 2005. In terms of units, 10 500 cars were exported in 1997 and this grew to 97 300 in 2001. It is expected that this will grow further to 153 000 in 2003. That's roughly 39 per cent growth per year.

In Japan, Daimler-Chrysler has enough confidence in our country to promote its vehicles, manufactured in East London, as 'Made in South Africa'.

Efficiency has increased too. In 1994, it took 112 hours to assemble an average vehicle in South Africa, whereas by 1999 this had been reduced to sixty hours. Unfortunately, this still isn't good enough, since the European benchmark is twenty hours, but we are headed in the right direction. Importantly, the improved efficiency hasn't been at the expense of quality. In 2002, a US-based global marketing information services company awarded BMW's plant outside Pretoria the European Gold Plant Quality Award, ranking it first among European plants for quality. BMW's plant in Germany received only a Silver award, while Daimler Chrysler's German plant got a Bronze award.

BMW, Daimler Chrysler and Volkswagen export cars all over the world and they continue to look for new markets. While these three companies build about 97 per cent of South Africa's car exports to the USA, Japan, Europe and Australasia, Toyota is also getting in on the act. Toyota is planning to invest R3.5 billion in its South African operations over the next four years, and intends to export between 15 000 and 20 000 Corollas to Australia from March 2003.

The export of automotive components has also grown rapidly, with an average annual growth of 33 per cent being maintained over the past six years. The growth has been mainly in catalytic converters, with exports increasing from R4.7 billion in 2000 to R9 billion in 2001. Delta Motor Corporation, which does not export whole vehicles at all, increased its export turnover from R304 million in 1997 to R2.05 billion in 2001, through components alone.

Shooting stars

The film industry has also experienced dramatic growth since 1994. The estimated value of the industry to metropolitan Cape Town alone, which is the Hollywood of South Africa, is R2 billion a year. In 2000, Cape Town issued permits for about 820 film shooting days, which compares well with San Francisco's 980 shooting days. Much of the boom has been due to advertisements made for British, German and US companies. However, South Africa is also being discovered by some of the bigger film companies now, and stars Bruce Willis, Val Kilmer and LL Cool J have come to Cape Town to work on their latest movies.

Foreigners are attracted by the Cape's beauty and diversity – it is possible to film in a variety of locations, from beaches and mountains to vineyards and cityscapes, all within an hour of each other. It is also very easy to disguise Cape Town as a European or American city – the Bo Kaap substitutes for San Francisco's steep streets, Camps Bay for the beaches of Florida, Plett's waves stand in for California's and Stellenbosch for the vineyards of southern France. Producers are also mindful that filming in Cape Town is twenty per cent cheaper than in Australia, and thirty to forty per cent cheaper than in Europe or the USA. Added to this, we have a growing number of state-of-the-art production studios and a pool of well-trained, experienced film crews and actors.

The growth of the film industry in Cape Town is already on a par with the take-off of tourism. This expansion has been achieved with virtually no government support, unlike competitive locations like Canada, Australia and India, which give their movie-makers very favourable incentives. Imagine what might be achieved if government incentives are put in place, not only for the film industry and its supporting businesses like car hire and catering, but also the spin-offs from increased exposure and tourism, as South African locations are featured in movies around the globe.

High spirits

The South African wine industry has had a proud tradition since the introduction of vines by Dutch and French immigrants more than 300 years ago. The nineteenth century Cape Constantia white wines were mentioned in her books by

Victorian author Jane Austen, and Vin de Constance from Klein Constantia was reputed to be the favourite drink of Napoleon. More recently, since the end of South Africa's isolation period, our wines are once again enjoying global recognition. For example, at Queen Elizabeth's jubilee celebrations in June 2002, VIP guests attending the garden party outside Buckingham Palace all received dinky bottles of Nederburg wine in their gourmet picnic hampers. Our wines are also regularly winning international awards and once again finding their way into the best restaurants around the world.

This new-found success is no coincidence. Our wine industry has literally been reinvented. Thirty years ago, there were 23 wine estates and thirty wholesale wine producers in the Western Cape. The *John Platter Guide*, widely regarded as the bible of the Cape wine industry, now lists around 4 000 wines from seventy wine cooperatives, and reviews nearly 150 wine cellars, exporters and wholesalers. Included are sixteen wines classified in the five-star 'superlative' category. Simply put, the industry has gone world-class. South African wine-makers have studied and practised in France, California and Australia. New, often foreign, owners have taken over estates and invested in new technologies, cultivars and expertise. Wine-makers have become more innovative and are using local cultivars like pinotage in dazzling new ways.

Pinotage, a wine enjoyed all over the world, is made from a grape cultivar created in 1925 by Professor Al Peroldt of the University of Stellenbosch.

As a result of all this, exports of South African wines grew by 24 per cent in 2001 – three times the average annual growth rate of the previous four years. KWV, the co-operative that used to be the industry regulator but which is now an unlisted public company, almost doubled its earnings in 2001/02. This has been largely attributed to a forty per cent increase in its foreign sales, about half of which came through increased volume and the rest through the depreciation of the rand.

Exports of other agricultural products are also growing by the year. Exports of South African fruit to Russia more than doubled between 2000 and 2001, and are expected to almost double again in 2002. If the Russians decide to re-classify South Africa as a developing country, the prospects look even better for the future.

Minerals continue to be a big money-spinner for our economy. For example, South Africa is now the largest exporter of unfinished diamonds (regardless of where they are mined) to the USA. This business grew by sixty per cent in 2001. We have now outstripped our major competitors – the UK and Belgium used to have an equal market share with us. Platinum is another mining success story, with an eighty per cent increase in export sales in 2001.

And let's not forget the smaller companies, like the winner of the 2002 Cape Town Regional Chamber of Commerce & Industry's Maersk Sealand Exporter of the Year competition, Blue Bay Concepts, which has doubled its turnover every year for seven years, mainly through exports of the Rogz for Dogz pet products that make up eighty per cent of its production.

Challenges on the road ahead

In the light of all these positive developments, we have good reason to be bullish on the economic front. The government's prudent policies are helping to grow the economy responsibly, other countries want to trade with us, confidence is increasing, and our exports are booming. However, we must not forget that there are significant challenges that lie on the road ahead. Chief among these is HIV/AIDS. We must work together to address this problem, both on a personal and corporate level, so that we can prevent some of the worst predictions from coming true. Other challenges include an unacceptably high unemployment rate and the massive disparity in incomes.

Progress on these issues needs to be rapid and visible, and solutions found if we are to avoid any greater opposition to the government's commitment to its current economic strategy. We will also need to attract, train and retain skilled resources to take the economy to the next level. At the same time, we cannot become complacent about our competitors, like Brazil, China, India, and other countries in South America and South-East Asia, that are vying for the same foreign trade and investment. We need to keep an eye on what they are doing successfully and make sure that we do it better. Indeed, South Africa's political miracle will be a short-lived victory if it is not accompanied by an economic miracle. Such a miracle has already begun to manifest itself in this country, not least through our world-class companies and entrepreneurs, which we discuss in the next chapter.

5 Homegrown, world class

Not too many people would disagree that South Africa's natural beauty rivals some of the best in the world. But how many believe that we can compete (and win) internationally on the business front too? Far too often we hear people droning on about our unproductive workforce (despite the fact that South Africans get snapped up by employers overseas because of their work ethic), the inefficiencies of our service industry (despite the fact that South Africa's financial and hospitality industries receive some of the best service ratings in the world) and the negative impact of our affirmative-action policies (despite the fact that these have produced remarkable new talent and innovation and are essential for our long-term success).

This chapter rejects the pervasive national inferiority complex and shows how South Africa is already on the global map with companies and individuals that are world class. The late 1990s saw a trend of South African companies going global, outgrowing their parochial origins and starting to compete with the biggest and best anywhere. Companies like Anglo American, BHP Billiton, De Beers, Dimension Data, Investec, Lonmin, Old Mutual, Sasol and SABMiller.

Our country has also produced its fair share of rags-to-riches stories – our own African version of the American Dream. These are remarkable individuals who continually beat the odds of their humble beginnings and overcome prejudice to become role-model entrepreneurs. They are proof that the African Renaissance is not just a dream but a reality in the making. They remind us that individuals can and do make a difference.

From fishes into whales

South Africa is a small fish in a big pond as far as the world is concerned. We make up less than one per cent of the global population and a similar proportion of the world's economy. Yet, in the past five years, some of our homegrown organisations have mushroomed into giants in global terms. Some are even Fortune 500 global companies, like BHP Billiton (ranked 281 in revenue terms), Anglo American (ranked 341) and Old Mutual (ranked 453). These companies, along with SABMiller (formerly South African Breweries), are also FTSE 100 companies. In other words, they are amongst the 100-biggest stocks on the London Stock Exchange. Several others are not far behind, being listed on the FTSE top 250 companies, including Lonmin and Dimension Data.

Clearly, we are learning to box above our weight. The scale of some of these companies' operations bears this out. For example, BHP Billiton, now with operations in Africa, Asia, North America, South America and Australia, is the world's largest exporter of energy (thermal) coal, the world's largest exporter of hard-coking coal for the steel industry and the world's third- largest producer of iron ore. They are also major players in oil, gas, liquefied natural gas, nickel, diamonds and silver. Old Mutual, with £143 billion of funds under management around the Group at the end of 2001, is now one of the top forty asset managers in the world. In the USA, they are one of the top ten fixed- annuity businesses.

South African Breweries was the first international brewer to enter Central America (in November 2001), and has become the largest brewer and soft-drinks bottler there. In 2002, South African Breweries bought Miller Brewing from Phillip Morris to become

The world's largest:

mining company – BHP Billiton

diamond company – De Beers

platinum producer – Anglo American Platinum

Each has South African origins.

SABMiller. It is now the world's second-largest brewer, behind Anheuser Busch, the makers of Budweiser. SABMiller operates 111 breweries in 24 countries, employing over 38 000 people around the world, with 2001 production volumes in excess of 120-million hectolitres. In China, SABMiller is the second-largest and most-profitable brewer, with 27 breweries and a combined capacity of more than 31-million hectolitres. The company's Ibhayi brewery in South Africa can produce 2.3-million hectolitres per year, run by a shift of just thirteen people, at a capital cost of just US$47 per hectolitre. SABMiller also has extensive interests in non-alcoholic drinks businesses and casinos around the world. It is the world's largest bottler and distributor of Coca-Cola products outside the USA This is an extremely powerful global company, one that has built itself up over a hundred years of operations in South Africa, and is now expanding into virtually every area of the world.

Investec, which is another rapidly growing South African company, started from humble beginnings in 1974 as a small finance company in Johannesburg. In 2001 it was voted by *The Banker* as the fourth most-global company in the world for the second year running. Over the past ten years, it has registered compound annual growth in headline earnings per share in excess of 28 per cent. Similarly, Dimension Data was started as a small networking company in the 1980s by a group of school friends, and it has since spread its wings to establish operations in over thirty countries, and on six continents.

Sasol is another South African company with ambitious global aspirations, backed by the unique, patented Fischer-Tropps technology. Already, its expansion drive has led to the acquisition of chemical plants in Germany, Italy, the Netherlands and the USA. Sasol Mining received the international coal company of the year award in the 2002 Platts-Business Week Global Awards. Sasol Mining MD Riaan Rademan said: 'Despite the country's often difficult geological conditions and the severe competition from some of the world's other leading coal producers – notably from Australia and the US – Sasol has demonstrated that South Africans can rival international best-business and mining practices.'

Sasol was the world's first petroleum-from-coal refinery and provides forty per cent of South Africa's petrol. The company Sasol now competes globally in the energy industry.

These are just some examples of companies that are led by incredibly-driven South Africans with big dreams of taking African excellence to the world, and who are succeeding.

Children of the African Dream

In addition to these awakening corporate giants, we have incredible entrepreneurs in our country. In fact, we seem to be a breeding ground for the spirit of innovation. Take Jabulane Mabuza, for instance, who went from university dropout to taxi driver to businessman to Chairman of African Renaissance Holdings, CEO of Tsogo Sun Holdings and MD of Southern Sun Gaming Investments. Or our retail granddaddy, Raymond Ackerman, who bought four very small supermarkets in 1967 and turned them into the multi-billion-rand family supermarket chain, Pick 'n Pay, which now also operates seventy stores in

Australia. The Rupert family has taken on the world too – through Rembrandt and Richemont. The latter is now ranked the second largest producer of luxury consumer goods in the world, after LVMH Moët Hennessy Louis Vuitton, and its stable includes brands such as Cartier, Cleef & Arpels, Piaget and Montblanc.

How many people know the name, Zutulele KK Combi? He started out owning a spaza shop in Guguletu in Cape Town and used his earnings to build the township's first petrol station. His success allowed him to build the Nyanga Junction shopping centre, which he later sold to Southern Life for R45 million. Not one to sit back on his laurels, he went on to create Master Currency and now controls ten per cent of the South African foreign exchange market. In 2000, he was named South Africa's Best Entrepreneur and, in 2001, he won the Ernst & Young World Entrepreneur of the Year Award for Managing Change. His advice to other budding entrepreneurs is to 'be tenacious, stay focussed, be passionate and be prepared for hard work.' Clearly, his formula pays off!

Liz McGrath is another of our world-class business people. She began by converting a 'run-down sleepy hollow' into the Look-Out Hotel in South Africa's Plettenberg Bay, and today her portfolio of luxury hotels includes, among others, The Cellars-Hohenhort on the slopes of Table Mountain and The Marine in the coastal town of Hermanus. She has been lauded as one of the top businesswomen in the world by a host of organisations, including *Fortune* magazine. Her philosophy on life is to 'be perpetually optimistic and always bear in mind that you are only as good as your team.'

A great source of South African entrepreneurial biographies is Mike Lipkin and Reg Lascaris' book, *Fire & Water*, which profiles people like Khethla Mthembu, Herman Mashaba, Anant Singh, Don Ncube and Hylton Appelbaum. Theirs are inspiring tales of self-belief and faith in South Africa and its people. Not surprisingly, each of them is highly motivated in their quest, not only to grow successful businesses, but also to empower a nation. For some, like Mthembu, founder of insurance company AFGEN and head of New Age Beverages, and Ncube, chairman of New Africa Investment Holdings, the drive is economic empowerment and eliminating black peoples' historically-entrenched inferiority complex in the business world. For others, like Mashaba, originator of the Black Like Me haircare brand, or internationally-acclaimed film producer, Anant Singh, the empowerment concerns embracing and celebrating our unique African-ness. Still others have focussed their creativity on tackling the specific challenges of Africa, like Appelbaum's support for the batteryless wind-up radio and the wind-up torch (invented by Briton Trevor Baylis).

The art of success

It's not just mega-companies that we have to be proud of either. South Africa has a growing number of individuals and small businesses making a success out of their own creativity in the 'functional-art' market. This term can be credited to one of the most successful and well-known of these functional artists, Carrol Boyes, who is famous for her extraordinary, quirky creations in pewter. Her kitchen utensils, cutlery, office items and ornaments can be found in homes and offices across North America, Europe, Asia and Australia. Boyes realised that if she was going to survive as an artist she needed to fuse her art with something that people would find useful. Today, she has more than a thousand pieces in her very distinctive range. Production has increased from an initial 400 pieces per month to around 40 000 pieces, and she employs over 450 people.

Dolosse – large concrete shapes which are used all over the world to protect harbour walls and watercraft from wave action – were designed in South Africa by Eric Merrifield.

Many of our most entrepreneurs can also be found plying their trade on the bustling pavements of our cities or in the burgeoning craft markets that are mushrooming all over the country. Streetwires is one such business. Street-wire art is unique to southern Africa – born in the shantytowns and on dusty backroads and baptised on the street, this genre is today a thriving and legitimate art form in its own right. Streetwires' motto is 'Anything you can dream up in wire, we can build' … and they do: a full spectrum of creatures great and small, Christmas trees and baobab trees, cars and motor bikes (even down to specific models), radios and light shades … anything!

Another craft-oriented success story is the Monkey Business Bead Project, which markets beaded dolls made by township artisans. They have gone from an idea inspired by the Grahamstown Arts Festival in 1994, to a trio of pioneering beadworkers in 2000, to 140 artists in 2002 supplying 25 retail outlets in South Africa and five international agents placing dolls with dealers in New York and London. Then there is the T-Bag Design Project, which has allowed a group of formally-unemployed women in Hout Bay's Imizamo Yethu informal settlement to break into the international scene by creating greeting cards with African designs painted onto discarded tea bags. They have had orders from Liberty of London and the South African Embassy in France, and they have made menus for functions held at the SA Reserve Bank. Currently, they throw the tea-leaves away and use only the bags, but they are also considering making designer paper with the leaves.

By showing such amazing initiative, our masters of wire, beads and recycling are not only creating much-needed employment, but are also playing their part in creating a distinctive brand for South Africa among tourists and overseas buyers.

How do many of our up-and-coming entrepreneurs get their products to these foreign markets? Look no further than www.buysouthafricaonline.com. The winner of the 2002 Development Marketplace Innovation Competition of the World Bank, Buy South Africa Online has developed a web-based system for small manufacturers to deal directly with the end-consumers of their products. By streamlining the supply chain, small traders in South Africa obtain a fairer share of the final sale price. Of course, many of these small traders do not have access to the Internet. No problem! Buy South Africa Online has addressed the digital divide by enabling remotely-located entrepreneurs to receive their orders automatically by SMS on a cell-phone, thereby bypassing the need for expensive computer equipment and training.

The Kreepy Krauly automatic pool cleaner, now world-famous, was invented in South Africa in 1974 by hydraulics engineer Ferdi Chauvier.

Lessons in radical innovation

Lessons in Radical Innovation is the title of a book by Wolfgang Grulke, the subtitle of which is 'South Africans leading the world'. It is about real people who took risks, who set themselves extraordinary goals at almost impossible odds, and succeeded. It contains stories about out-of-the-box thinking, passionate individuals and the different kinds of companies they created. They are entrepreneurs who have combined innovation with technology to create a massively-disruptive cocktail, which is precisely Grulke's formula for radical innovation. In this section, we highlight just two of the stories in the book – about Johnnic and Chef Works – but we recommend that you get a copy and read about other inspiring South African innovators.

In the space of a few short years in the 1990s, Johnnic was transformed from a lumbering, monolithic company mining minerals and manufacturing goods into a focussed, dynamic company 'mining' information and 'manufacturing' news. This metamorphosis rivals Finnish company Nokia's change from a pulp-and-paper manufacturer into a world leader in cellular technology and French company

Vivendi's creation of a global-media magnate from the ashes of a waste-and-water company. Perhaps we should not be surprised considering that the task fell to the man who was one of the alchemists behind South Africa's miraculous political transformation, Cyril Ramaphosa. Today, Johnnic houses a family of media, communication and entertainment assets, from newspapers (Sunday Times, Sowetan Sunday World and I-Net Bridge) and television/film (M-Net, Cartoon Network and Nu Metro), to mobile-phone networks (MTN) and books and publishers (Exclusive Books, Random House and Struik).

And that's only half the story. The other half is the way in which Johnnic is creating world-beating technologies, like Remote Interactive Voice Response, which is being marketed around the world as the 'New, Better Thing' by Unisys, the American IT giant. 'When we showed it to Unisys,' says M-Cell CEO Paul Edwards, 'all they could do was slap their foreheads and say, 'Why didn't we think of this?' It's such a simple, easy alternative to WAP (Wireless Application Protocol) and it works. Everyone out there was thinking so far forward that they missed a solution that was staring them in the face.' MTN also serves as the SMS (Short Message Service) gateway for PC-to-mobile messaging for AOL (America Online), the world's biggest Internet service provider. The data comes down the network from Chicago to Johannesburg, is reformatted into SMS and then sent out to about 120 countries. 'There's none of the ten-year lag anymore,' says Edwards. 'The stuff we're doing, the technology we're producing, is leading-edge. We're at the forefront. We're connected.'

'What excites me most is the fact that what we're doing down here is what guys are still trying to do in Europe and America.'

Paul Edwards
CEO, SA telecommunications company, M-Cell

Thinking outside the box has become a way of life in South Africa, and it is what turned South African family company, Chef Works, from a mature, declining manufacturer of traditional, white clothing for restaurants and hotels, into a global company that is now the hottest, hippest supplier in the hospitality-clothing game. Deciding that their only chance of survival was to break into the American market, they realised they would have to get 'funky and outrageous', which is exactly what defines their in-demand brand today – brightly coloured designs swirling with red-hot chilli peppers, jungle-green jalapeños, twirling spaghetti, French mushrooms and flashy chopping utensils. By 2001, they had more than 30 000 customers in

America alone, supplying major hotel groups, casinos, cruiselines and restaurants. Other orders are pouring in from Canada, England, Europe, Australia, New Zealand, Singapore, Japan, the Middle East and Africa. 'It's been amazing to me,' says co-owner Alan Gross, 'that we as a South African company could even think of selling our goods overseas. I mean, we're a mature South African business. We always thought we'd be able to make a living and educate our children. We always thought we understood the boundaries. Suddenly, the whole picture changes radically. Suddenly, we're global. Suddenly, everything is different.'

The great advantage of coming from South Africa is that our recent history has shaken us up. Everything is in flux. We expect constant change and that is good for innovation, because as the old saying goes, 'Creativity emerges from chaos'. New York at the end of the 1800s was filled with newly-arrived immigrants with radical fresh ideas, nothing stable about their lives and not much to lose. For the next four decades it was the energetic centre of the world's creative thinkers and innovators. South Africa is the new 'Wild West'. The radical ideas are coming from right here, because people are willing to take risks and see things in new ways. That is the nature of such an unsettled environment with so much opportunity. No wonder *Newsweek* magazine, in September 2002, voted Cape Town as one of the world's eight most creative cities, along with others like Austin (USA), Tijuana (Mexico), Zhongguancun (China) and Kabul (Afghanistan).

Closing the digital divide

Someone who seems never to have understood boundaries is Mark Shuttleworth, whose meteoric rise to fame and fortune is the stuff of legends in South Africa. A straight-A graduate from the University of Cape Town, Mark followed his passion in 1996 by setting up a small Internet consulting company called Thawte. Thawte rapidly found its niche by taking an innovative approach to digital certification, earning forty per cent of the market and US$90 000 a month by 2000, at prices that were two-thirds lower than their biggest competitor, VeriSign. The following year, Shuttleworth sold the business to VeriSign for US$575 million, making him a 26-year-old billionaire in his home country. Famously, he gave R1 million to each of his sixty employees (including two cleaners and a gardener), and set up a venture-capital company for South African entrepreneurs called Here be Dragons, before paying US$20 million to become the world's second civilian astronaut (and first Afro-naut). He dismisses his success as 'the usual suspects: luck, timing, foolhardy bravery in the face of insurmountable odds, inspiration, perspiration, blood, sweat and tears.' He admits to being driven by a core philosophy, which is to put passion ahead of practicality: 'if you do what you love, you will love what you do. Then you'll do it better than anybody who's just doing it as a job. And as long as you have the wisdom to keep doing it for love rather than for money, it will never be spoiled for you.'

The Shuttleworth-style technological leadership should not be regarded as the exception in South Africa. There are many others who are closing the digital divide. Consider this list of world firsts, with a South African twist, compiled by Ken Jarvis, CEO of Idion Solutions:

- Saswitch was the world leader in allowing remote ATM access by any institution with any institution, regardless of network protocol. The next country anywhere in the world took over five years to launch a similar service;
- Nedcor was the first bank anywhere in the world to strategise and implement Microsoft technology on teller platforms;
- Standard Bank was a pioneer in the world of banking by allowing 'securitisation' of an asset online to gain access to funds in other environments by using Access Bond;
- UBS was the first bank in the world to use IMS Fastpath for simplified banking transactions, allowing it, at that stage, to process more transactions per second than any other bank working with similar volumes;
- Outside the financial-services industry, Computicket's technology for providing online ticketing across multiple geographic locations and for multiple venues and categories, was a world first;
- Multichoice was the second company in the world to launch satellite TV;
- Paul Maritz, the man behind the global NT software, is a graduate of the University of Cape Town and the University of Natal, where he studied computer science and mathematics;
- Ivan Epstein, CEO of Softline, started with R5 000; today, Softline provides accounting software in eight languages and in over 38 countries;
- Incredible Connection is the largest IT retailer to the public in South Africa and achieved this only six years after being founded; and,
- Omnipless, launched in 1994, manufactures world-class antennas in a niche market for satellite communication, and nearly one hundred per cent of its product is exported.

Most recently, a start-up company called Viamedia scored another world first when it released idj with itouch, South Africa's SMS and cellphone-technology whizz-kids. idj allows radio listeners to call a number and listen to the song they have just heard on the radio, hear the rest of the album and order the CD. Music lovers can even send a song to a friend. Through itouch's international network, the service will soon be introduced around the world.

Another technology pioneer is a small Stellenbosch-based company called Electronic Development House (EDH) Marketing, which recently secured a three-year rolling contract with the Association of Tennis Professionals. This group runs 67 tournaments in more than thirty countries, and EDH will supply its innovative electronic scoring system. In 2002 the system was used to score games at Wimbledon. Soon, they will integrate the 'Rocket Radar' into the system, which accurately measures the ball's trajectory, racquet-head speeds and the speed of the ball off the racquet. Other products developed by EDH include the 'Speedball' cricket-bowling speed-measurement device that is used in South Africa and around the world, and a golf radar system that records the trajectory and carry of the ball immediately after it has been struck.

Incubator for entrepreneurs

There are countless more South African companies that have found global niches and are growing to become world leaders in their field. We cite here just a few more, in case you are not yet convinced:

- The Steinhoff Group has 53 factories within South Africa and is the largest furniture producer in the Southern Hemisphere.
- In a recent project, Sapekoe began the development of one of the world's first organic tea farms.
- Afrikelp has devised a way to produce environmentally-friendly organic fertiliser from kelp (seaweed).
- Gelvenor Textiles is the leading global producer of hi-tech, specialist fabrics for niche markets. It was the world's first company to produce products for people suffering from incontinence.

Dr Christiaan Barnard performed the world's first heart transplant in Cape Town on 3 December 1967. More than 50 000 similar operations have since been performed all over the world.

- SAPY produced the world's first 'soft-feel' polypropylene yarn.
- SANS developed a unique, revolutionary new product to add colour to polyester, called Colorcord, which is also environmentally friendly. In 2002, SANS cornered almost 75 per cent of the world market in industrial yarn and is seeking to become the sole supplier of nylon thread to Nike.

- The Pratley Group, best known for Pratley's Putty, own three hundred patents worldwide.
- RGR Technologies has designed and produced a valve, used in the mining industry, to pump water from depths of four to five kilometres below the surface, making it the only company producing this product in the world and exporting it globally.

South Africa is an incubator for entrepreneurs, like those that we have mentioned above. Growing numbers of companies around the world are starting to recognise this unique strength in South Africa, as did global accounting firm Deloitte & Touche Tohmatsu, when they headquartered their Innovation Zone here, under the executive leadership of Louis Geeringh. Explaining their rationale in *Radical Innovation*, Geeringh says that 'most innovation seems to occur at the edge of the empire – away from the controls, the corporate governance and the emperor. When all the odds are against you and you have to do things out of necessity to stay in business, as is the case with South Africa, it breeds a certain type of hunger in people – an essential nutrient to make innovation flourish.'

South African physicist Allan Cormack and Sir Godfrey Hounsfield of EMI Laboratories in the United Kingdom, developed the CAT scan.

It is not only world-class business entrepreneurs that South Africa has managed to cultivate. There are individuals who have excelled across the full range of science, art and culture.

Our four Nobel Peace Prize winners are fairly well known (and we discuss them in a later chapter), but did you know that we also have two Nobel Laureates for Physiology or Medicine? They are Max Theiler, for his discoveries concerning yellow fever and how to combat it (1951), and Allan M Cormack and Sir Godfrey Hounsfield, for the development of the computed axial tomography scan (1979). In the same field, we should not forget Dr Christiaan Barnard, who performed the world's first successful heart transplant at Groote Schuur Hospital in Cape Town, in 1967. The operating theatre in which this historic event took place is now a museum.

In addition to Mahatma Gandhi (who we also talk about later), there is another world leader who was not South African, but who forged his ideas here. Britain's Lord Robert Baden Powell's innovative use of young boys as messengers, lookouts, runners, signallers and first-aid attendants during the historic 217-day siege of Mafeking (now called Mafikeng) during the South African War, led to him establishing the worldwide movement of Boy Scouts and Girl Guides. Today, there are more than 25 million Scouts – young and adult, boys and girls – in 216 countries and territories.

Pioneers of the triple bottom line

Much of this chapter has been about being 'bigger than' or 'best at' in terms of products and profits. In keeping with its hosting of the UN World Summit on Sustainable Development, however, South Africa is also beginning to show its leadership in the so-called 'triple bottom line' – balancing the needs of prosperity (economy) with people (society) and the planet (environment).

Sonop wine estate, based in Paarl in the Western Cape, is one of many role models in this respect. A *Business Day* article referred to it as being a good example of 'fermenting change'. Sonop is the only South African winery producing significant quantities of organic wine for export, approximately 45 000 cases a year. Having converted sixty per cent of the 75 hectares of land under vines into organic production, with the remaining forty per cent under conversion, the farm now supplies more than ten per cent of the total wines exported from South Africa.

KWV (the Ko-operatiewe Wijnbouwers Vereniging) owns the largest wine cellar in the world. The cellar in Paarl covers an area of 24 hectares and has a storage capacity of 121-million litres of wine.

There are social, economic and environmental benefits to the organic approach, including being labour intensive, environmentally friendly and satisfying a growing. This embraces the classic 'triple bottom line' of sustainability. From an economic perspective, not only are organic exported wines sold at a premium, but demand exceeds supply on both local and international markets. And the market itself is expanding from Europe to the UK and USA.

The bulk of the export volume stems from the Winds of Change label, which funds an empowerment initiative, the Mountain View Communal Property Association. For each case of wine sold, a percentage is given to the association, which in turn funds various pilot projects like adult literacy and the construction of community facilities.

Sonop is also an experiment in land reform. In 2000, the farm sold ten hectares of land to eighteen workers for R400 000. Of this land, eight hectares have been planted with vines and the remainder is used for residential purposes. With the government land-grant scheme, which gave R16 000 to each family, and the funds ploughed into the association by the Winds of Change label, the farm is able to fund other social initiatives, such as an educare centre and health-care training.

Andries Lotter, chairman of the Association, reflects on the positive changes, saying, 'After we became land owners, we began to see many changes taking place. We are part of the decision-making process now, and feel very proud of what we have, of where we are. There is a tight community spirit. We are like a family on this farm.'

Spier wine estate, in Stellenbosch, is showing a similar appetite for sustainable development. Former farm labourers have been given an ownership and management stake in the vineyards and vegetable farming enterprises. In addition, Spier has embarked on establishing an off-site eco-village, which will eventually incorporate schools, offices, craft workshops, an arts venue, a community centre and homes for almost 150 local families. Apart from environmentally-friendly materials and design, the eco-village is also piloting a world-leading solar energy column technology.

There have been various ecological reforms at Spier as well. With 140 hectares of land set aside for organic farming, it is now one of the largest commercial organic farms in South Africa, cultivating both vegetables and vines. Spier has also formed a subsidiary called Green Technologies, which acquired the South African licence for an environmentally-friendly waste treatment system called the Biolytix Filter. The installation of this Biolytic Filtration system at The Village at Spier is the first of its kind on this scale in the world. Other features include a cheetah education centre, an open air amphitheatre and an Arts Trust that showcases local talent.

For the people, by the people

Our final homegrown success story in this chapter tackles education. The need for tertiary education in South Africa is profound. Only six per cent of South Africans have any tertiary education at all. In fact, in the black population, the figure is only three per cent. CIDA is a model for making a quantum-leap of a difference in tackling this issue in South Africa.

CIDA City Campus is the first virtually-free university-level institution in South Africa. CIDA offers three times the hours of high-quality university-level education at a tenth of the cost, and is achieving extraordinary results in both academic and secular activities. Eighty per cent of the 1 600 students come from rural areas and twenty per cent from townships, squatter camps and inner-city areas. Yet the pass rate for first years is 75 per cent.

All this is possible through extensive innovation. The campus is managed by the students, allowing them to learn and get work experience simultaneously while studying. Students do administration work, computer maintenance, admissions, marketing, computer training and even run the canteen. CIDA does not employ academics – the belief is that skills and knowledge are best transferred by those who use them daily, and therefore volunteer industry experts deliver the curriculum. The intention is to produce workplace-ready graduates and entrepreneurs.

CIDA's motto for students is that they do not come to CIDA as individuals, 'they come as a village.' Every one of the students has an important responsibility to help build their local or rural community. They play a bridging role between the First World economy and their world. In agreement with the principals of the feeder schools, CIDA students go back into their home-based school with a well-managed extra-curricula programme on economic literacy. This focusses on money management, savings, credit, business training and general management. In 2001 there were 1 200 CIDA students involved in this programme in 1 000 schools, a programme that reaches over a million high school students. Soon, CIDA will have 2 200 students reaching over two million young people.

According to Founder Teddy Blecher, who gave up a lucrative career as an actuary to start up the university, 'Research, which compares the success of First and Third World nations, has proven that there is a ninety per cent correlation between higher education and a country's achievements. For South Africa to become globally competitive, it is vital that this homegrown mass-scale higher education is a success.'

It is the truly world-class initiatives like CIDA, tackling South Africa's most pressing needs like educational upliftment in a creative way, that give us plenty of hope for the future.

6 Wild, beautiful and free

South Africa is a wild land of awesome beauty and spectacular contrasts. There is nothing monotonous or homogenous about this land or its people. South Africa powerfully engages the senses – the sights, the sounds, the tastes and the smells are always different and always intense.

There are landscapes ranging from scorching deserts to snow-capped mountains, varied vegetation from lush yellowwood forests to hardy Karoo scrub, and fauna of every description, from the mighty African elephant to its miniature cousin, the dassie. In the Cape, the seasons bring violent winter rainstorms and hot, dry summers, while the rest of the country experiences warm, soaking summer rains and cold, parched winters. The sun is always shining somewhere in South Africa, no matter what day of the year it is! The west coast is lapped by the icy waters brought north from Antarctica by the Benguela current, while the east coast has the enticing warm tropical Mozambique current. Each supports its own unique marine environment. Culturally, an intoxicating mix of African, European and Asian influences infuse the country's languages, religions, music, cuisine, art and architecture.

South Africa truly represents the world in one country. In this chapter, we take a look at some of what we have on offer in our own unique corner of the world, from the blessings that nature has bestowed upon us, to the richness of our heritage and the special global niches being carved out by our tourism industry. This goes some way to explaining the tremendous growth in foreign tourist numbers, and reminds us how much there is to do and see right here at home.

Blessings of nature

Africa has an extraordinary abundance of natural riches on land, in the sea and in the air. These haven't always been appreciated or conserved as well as they should have, but it is heartening to know that, in South Africa, the government has recognised our natural heritage as a unique asset to be preserved and developed for the enjoyment of current and future generations. South Africans have also spotted the massive economic opportunities presented by eco-tourism, one of the fastest-growing segments of the tourism industry. We currently have over three million hectares reserved for conservation, and this is growing year-by-year.

Sanctuary for wildlife

South Africa has some 403 protected areas, ranging from the massive and world-renowned Kruger National Park (established in 1898, it is larger than Israel and is one of the oldest and best-managed nature reserves in Africa), to the tiny and little-known Mkambati Nature Reserve in the Eastern Cape. Our wildlife populations are particularly well-managed and plentiful, and the reserves are easy to get to and move around in because of South Africa's excellent transport and accommodation infrastructure. This makes the country among the best places in the world to view big game. Many trophy seekers are also attracted by hunting opportunities in our carefully-controlled game reserves.

In the next twenty years, South African National Parks will expand the country's protected areas from six to eight per cent of the land's surface. During the same period, protected marine- and coastal-environmental areas will be expanded from five to twenty per cent. Already, Addo Elephant National Park in the Eastern Cape, which used to be one of the smallest of our national parks, has grown ten-fold to over 90 000 hectares. Now known as Greater Addo, it has become a 'Big Seven' park, featuring leopard, lion, elephant, rhino and buffalo (the traditional 'Big Five'), plus dolphins and whales.

Most tourists aim to see the 'Big Five', but we should also take pride in some of the smaller and no-less fascinating creatures that are found in our country. Foreign bird watchers, for instance, already bring between R10 million and R25 million into our economy each year. This is not surprising given that South Africa boasts over 900 species of birds.

A good deal of the phenomenal success of our wildlife conservation has been the result of visionary initiatives. Courageous people and institutions have pushed past the constraints of fear and negativity about South Africa's future, and come up with unique ways to develop nature conservation as a sustainable and lucrative industry for the future.

Adrian Gardiner, one of the nominees for the 2000 Audi Terra Nova Awards, is a classic example of such a person. He took 20 000 hectares of degraded farmland in the Eastern Cape and transformed it into one of the most biologically-diverse game reserves in the country, now famously known as Shamwari. In addition to planting indigenous pioneering grasses and reseeding the contours with shrubs and trees, he reintroduced 10 000 head of game in eight years. Many of the species had disappeared from the Cape region in the last few centuries. At first everyone thought he was crazy but, as the success of Shamwari has shown, sometimes crazy is actually visionary.

Paths of peace

A concept and approach that South Africa is pioneering, is community participation in wildlife conservation. For example, two new tribe-owned lodges have opened on the rim of the Kruger National Park – Phumulani, owned by the Mdluli tribe, and Wisani Lodge, owned by the Mhinga tribe. Community-based tourism proves that conservation and development do not have to be in conflict and we do not necessarily have to choose between people and animals. The organisation, Fair Trade in Tourism South Africa (FTTSA), embodies similar principles of sharing the benefits of tourism equitably with the local population.

South Africa has the second-highest waterfall in the world – the 850-metre high Tugela Falls in the Drakensberg in KwaZulu-Natal.

Another visionary initiative currently underway in South Africa is the creation of Transfrontier Conservation Areas, also known as Peace Parks, because of their role in improving cross-border relations between neighbouring countries. Six such parks have been proposed in southern Africa, including the Great Limpopo Transfrontier Park, which was created in 2002. The latter joins Mozambique's Coutada 16 Park, Zimbabwe's Gonarezhou Park and South Africa's Kruger National Park. This contiguous wilderness is 35 000 km^2 in extent, which makes it larger than some European countries!

Along similar lines, recognising that our tourism strength lies in cooperation as a region, two cross-border Spatial Development Initiatives (SDIs) have been launched. The Coast-to-Coast SDI started as a trucking route linking Mozambique on the east and Namibia on the west, via Swaziland, South Africa and Botswana. The tourism opportunities soon became clear, with the N4 highway taking visitors from Maputo, through subtropical Swaziland and Mpumalanga, Gauteng's cradle of humankind (and shopping basket), the game-rich Limpopo Province, across the sands of the Kalahari desert in Botswana and finally to the German coffee and café culture of Swakopmund. That's 3 000 kilometres of incredible, exotic Africa!

Oceans of plenty

In its August 2002 edition, *National Geographic* ran a wonderfully-ebullient story about 'South Africa's teeming seas', declaring that the 3 000 kilometres or so of South African coastline form 'one of the richest, most biologically-diverse and most oceanographically-complex marine environments on Earth – the Serengeti of the sea'. It is not surprising that tourists and locals alike are starting to discover a new kind of wildlife experience – 'water safaris' that take in the sights and sounds of whales, dolphins, sharks, penguins and colourful coral reefs.

As a result of the increasing numbers of whales visiting our shores since the international ban on whaling, the whale-watching industry has grown at a phenomenal rate and is already estimated to be worth around R500 million to the economy. Coastal communities such as Hermanus have turned this into a great tourist attraction, by employing a whale crier, a setting up a whale-watch hotline and putting on an annual whale festival.

In addition to whale-fever, Cape Town has for many years offered trips to the seal colonies along its coast. It is also hard to resist an up-close-and-personal encounter with hundreds of African penguins at one of three mainland penguin nesting sites. If cute and fluffy is not your style, False Bay is becoming famous for the unique behaviour of its Great White sharks, which breach or jump clear of the water in the same way that whales and dolphins do. Adrenaline junkies are queuing up to go cage diving with these predators.

Further up the east coast, it seems the most normal thing in the world to spot vast schools of dolphins, while in KwaZulu-Natal the annual sardine run, described by *National Geographic* as 'one of the marine wonders of the world', has spawned its own Sardine Festival in Scottburgh. And Sodwana Bay is poised to take over as a diving destination from more well-known diving meccas such as the Red Sea between Egypt and Israel.

It isn't only under the water where the action is happening. Let's not forget that other marine species – the surfer. South Africa's coast has some of the world's best surf and most of it is within easy access of the major cities. Dungeons, the big-wave surfing spot off Cape Town, is considered one of the six most important big-wave spots in the world. Certainly we are poised to benefit from the tremendous growth in global-surf tourism. The Quicksilver ISA World Surfing Games, held in Durban in 2002, is a sign of things to come.

Kingdom of flowers

One of South Africa's greatest treasures is still its floral bounty, specifically the Cape fynbos, which covers the smallest area but is the most diverse of the world's six floral kingdoms. There are more species of fynbos in the Western Cape than floral species in the whole of the United Kingdom. In fact, South Africa has more threatened plant species (around 3 000) than Europe's total plant species. Fortunately, the total species count is growing year by year – in 2000 alone, South African botanists discovered 60 new plant species, most of them fynbos.

It is not only fynbos with which we are blessed. Go up the west coast towards Springbok in the springtime and witness how the brown semi-desert landscape has burst into brightly-coloured carpets of endless yellow, orange and white Namaqualand daisies. Not too far down the track, in Niewoudtville, the soil is home to the largest variety of bulb species in the world. The streets of Los Angeles are lined with agapanthus and the city's official flower is the strelitizia, while flower pots in Europe are filled with hybrid geraniums – all flowers indigenous to South Africa. We have yet to fully capitalise on these floral assets commercially. Conversely, the bulb-growing Dutch earned more money in 2000 from the sale of South African indigenous bulbs than we redeemed in gold sales in the same year. Even so, the Cape wildflower industry alone is already worth R150 million a year, mostly in foreign exchange.

Elsewhere in the country, 150 000 hectares of the Waterberg has been declared one of the only savannah biosphere reserves in the world, and has been added to UNESCO's register of 386 global reserves in 91 countries. In addition to employing more than 1 500 people, it is one of the finest examples of biodiversity anywhere.

And it's not just our nature reserves that are green. Food and Trees for Africa claims that Johannesburg is one of the most treed cities in the world, and some even go far as to call it the world's largest forest created by humans. Certainly there are more bird species found in and around Johannesburg than ever before, as exotic immigrants such as the loerie and others have migrated there, drawn by the ever-greener environment.

Footprints of history

Many people, including apartheid-era textbook writers, seem to think that our history started in the 1600s, when in actual fact South Africa has an incredibly-rich history dating back to pre-human times and tracing the development of ancient advanced-African civilisations. Some of this history is still in the process of being discovered, and the rest of it is being carefully preserved and presented to take into account the important roles that all our people have played in shaping our nation and the world.

Cradle of humankind

Hidden beneath the surface of north-east Gauteng is the most complete and varied evidence of the origins of modern humans, known as the Cradle of Humankind. Embedded in rock in the 47 000 hectares around the dolomite Sterkfontein Caves, are the fossilised remains of hominids dating back over 3.3 million years. The site is home to world-famous Mrs Ples, the oldest complete hominid skeleton in the world, as well as the even older Littlefoot, which is still being excavated and studied.

The Cradle of Humankind was declared a World Heritage Site in December 1999, one of four in South Africa, along with Robben Island, the Drakensberg mountain reserve and the St Lucia Wetland Park. The Cradle is being developed into a major scientific and tourist centre. Interest is not restricted to palaeontology but includes the important archaeological sites of Stone Age and Iron Age periods. The full story of humanity is told on this single site. Not far away is the ancient Tswaing crater, evidence of an asteroid that struck the area more than two million years ago.

Bushmans Kloof Wilderness Reserve, a South African Natural Heritage Site with more than 125 rock-art sites, has been dubbed the world's largest open-air art gallery.

The arid Karoo in the Western Cape is also well known as a palaeontologist's heaven, as it is littered with pre-historic fossils. Most recently, footprints of an unbelievably-large scorpion – about the length of a human – were discovered in what used to be the muddy sediments of the ancient seabed of the Karoo around 260 million years ago. This is the largest trackway of an invertebrate yet found in the world, according to British scientist Dr John Almond, of Nature Viva.

Mapungubwe, where the Limpopo and Shashe Rivers meet in Limpopo Province, is another fascinating archaeological site. It is where a once-sophisticated ancient civilisation from Africa's Golden Age was based. A thousand years ago, when Europe was in the very depths of its dark ages, these African people were trading gold and ivory with China, Egypt and India, including delicate gold jewellery and finely-crafted pottery. Many of these cultural treasures are on permanent exhibition at the University of Pretoria, and the site is about to become the centrepiece of the planned Limpopo Shashe Transfrontier Conservation Area, between South Africa, Zimbabwe and Botswana.

South Africa's rich tapestry of rock art pre-dates the most visited temples and ruins around the world, and is by far the oldest record of human art, dating back around 10 000 years. This interpretation of the lives of our ancient ancestors is a gift that few other countries can offer to the world. The rock-art sites range from Bushmans Kloof Wilderness Reserve in the arid Cederberg, to Giant's Castle in the lush Drakensberg and Kaoxa Bush Camp in the riverine Limpopo Valley.

Bushmans Kloof, a South African Natural Heritage Site with more than 125 rock-art sites, has been dubbed the world's largest open-air art gallery. More than 20 000 individual San paintings have been counted in the vast expanse of the Drakensberg mountain range in KwaZulu-Natal. And on the Limpopo plains there are 2 000-year-old records of female-initiation friezes, diverse animal images and hunting scenes.

Colonial conquests

The arrival of the various colonial powers in Africa had a huge, irreversable impact on the traditional ways of life of the continent's indigenous populations. South Africa was no exception, as conquering Europeans added yet another dimension to our fascinating, turbulent history – the early settlers, the Great Trek, tribal conflicts, the South African wars, the diamond and gold rushes, the World Wars and apartheid. A rich architectural legacy survives to tell these stories, like the pentagonal Castle in Cape Town, beautiful Cape-Dutch homesteads overlooking wine estates in Stellenbosch and the grand Union Buildings in Pretoria. The introduction of Christian, Islamic, Jewish and Hindu faiths also resulted in the development of lovely old stone cathedrals, beautifully-crafted mosques, striking synagogues and magnificent temples.

We can also celebrate the interesting and dynamic fusion of African, European and Asian influences that makes us the cultural *potjie* that we are. One just has to visit the Grahamstown festival to witness that fusion at its most creative. Apart from our eleven official languages, some of the other languages that are also widely spoken around the country include Gudgerati, Hindi, Arabic, Hebrew, Greek, German, Portuguese and Italian. Our restaurants are increasingly using an unique and wonderful mixture of African ingredients and flavours and European methods of preparation, served up as tantalising and exotic treats. The décor in these restaurants, as well as in the hotels and game lodges around the country, is following the same trend, blending the best of European, Asian and African styles in an exciting, inviting and luxurious mix.

Struggles for freedom

In many ways, South Africa has been a land of struggle – for survival and freedom – by the Bushmen, the indigenous black tribes, and the Afrikaners, as well as the struggle against the apartheid system. For modern South Africans, there is the struggle against pervasive poverty and unacceptably-high levels of crime.

These struggles have moulded this country and its people. We may not be proud of everything that has transpired in our history, but it does make us uniquely South African, and it holds widespread interest for the rest of the world. Luckily, our new government did not go on a rampage to tear down icons of apartheid and rename virtually everything in honour of their own revolutionary leaders, as might have been expected. Instead, they have acknowledged these symbols as being an important part of our history and have transformed legacies of pain and suffering into symbols of liberation, that hold lessons for our future. As a result, the growing phenomenon of 'struggle tourism', to coin a phrase, can and should be embraced and showcased.

This heritage includes the Voortrekker Monument near Pretoria, which recalls, amongst other things, the victory of the Boers over the Zulus at the Battle of Blood River. Today, those same Boer commandos are recognised for having been fighters for freedom against British imperialism during the two South African Wars. Other sites include the Taal Monument in Paarl, the Huguenot Monument in Franschoek, the KwaMuhle Museum in Durban, the War Museum in Bloemfontein, the Hector Peterson Memorial in Soweto, the Apartheid Museum in Johannesburg, the Lilliesleaf Museum in Rivonia and the Robben Island Museum off the coast of Cape Town.

Each of these monuments and museums have fascinating stories to tell. Take Robben Island, for instance. There can be few islands in the world that have borne witness to as much suffering as this one, anchored off the coast of the Cape of Storms under the brooding gaze of Table Mountain. Over the centuries this tiny land has served as a place of isolation for lepers, common criminals and political prisoners.

Today, Robben Island has been recreated from a place synonymous with fear and loathing, into a symbol of strength and transformation. It lives on as a sobering monument to our bedevilled past, watched over by Ahmed Kathrada, a surviving member of the exclusive Robben Island 'Old Boy's Club', and run by former prisoners who now work as tour guides. The painful memories that haunt the bleak island are recounted in books like Kathrada's *Letters from Robben Island*, and Nelson Mandela's autobiography *Long Walk to Freedom*. For the tourist, whether conscientious, concerned or just curious, there must be few other places on the planet that are more infused with living history, culture and emotion.

In November 2001, the Apartheid Museum was opened to the public at Johannesburg's Gold Reef City. Quite apart from simply telling the story of one culture's domination over another, it manages to exude a sense of celebration at the transformation that this great country has undertaken. The museum's curator, Christopher Till, has witnessed the full gamut of reactions from visitors: from the white policeman tut-tutting about 'those terrible times', to ex-political prisoners breaking down in tears and schoolchildren awed into hushed whispers by their experience and asking, 'Did our parents really live through that?'

The rising tide of tourism

Having recognised the massive opportunities that our country and its culture present for tourism, South Africans are continuously learning from other tourist destinations and coming up with new and unique ways of providing foreigners with even more reasons to visit our shores. These range from the ever-popular and rapidly-growing adventure tourism, to safaris of a different kind – on the cosmetic surgeon's operating table!

It's a scream!

Over the years, New Zealand has become synonymous with adventure travel. However, with the sheer number of thrill-seeking options that South Africa can offer adrenalin-junkies, and our relatively-close proximity to Europe, this country is fast gaining a reputation as one of the premier destinations for this brand of tourism. It seems particularly attractive to the bold young backpackers who make their way overland through Africa.

The death-defying choices on offer in this country are mind-boggling: rollerblading in the annual Downhill Challenge down Kloof Nek in Cape Town, rock climbing in the Magaliesberg, abseiling and kloofing down the Storms River Gorge, surfing at one of the world's top-six big-wave spots at Dungeons off Hout Bay, rapp jumping (abseiling while facing the ground) from Johannesburg skyscrapers, kayaking on the Tugela River, paragliding from Lion's Head, hot-air ballooning over the Highveld, cage-diving with Great White sharks off the southern Cape, 4x4 trails into the mountains of Lesotho, or plunging from the world's highest commercial bungi-jump at the 216-metre Bloukranz Bridge.

In the lap of luxury

There is another kind of tourism that is apparently 'a scream'. Increasingly, wealthy tourists are combining a visit to South Africa with cosmetic surgery, be it laser-eye surgery, teeth-whitening, facelifts, nose-jobs, or breast enlargements. South Africa has first-rate medical centres, at prices that are literally unbeatable, and there are no waiting lists to speak of. Not only is it 'cheap', but it is discreet. Patients often spend their recovery time at an exclusive game park while the wounds and bruises heal. When they get home, they can tell their friends that the African air is great for rejuvenation! This so-called 'medical tourism' is an exploding phenomenon, and South Africa is perfectly positioned to become one of the world's leading destinations. Already, companies like Surgeons & Safaris can hardly keep pace with the demand.

For the less stressful tourist experience, we have the Cape winelands which are already the tenth most visited tourist attraction in South Africa. This is not only a great testimony to the quality of our 'nectar of the gods', which is growing in fame daily throughout the world, but also to the first-class creativity of the estates themselves. Over the past decade, wine farms have transformed themselves into must-see destinations. The experience now includes meandering

Singita Game Reserve, near the Kruger National Park, received a remarkable 100 per cent rating from the prestigious *Conde Nast* magazine as the best travel experience in the world, for 2001. In 2002, Singita was awarded the Purple Shield by Relais & Chateaux, and was voted 'Number 1 International Resort Hideaway in the World' for the second year, by the prestigious *Andre Harper's Hideaway Report*.

through the stunningly beautiful valleys of the Western Cape wine routes and casually stopping off at any number of famous estates for wine-tasting sessions, cellar tours, picnics, horse-drawn carriage excursions through the vineyards, candlelit dinners and luxurious overnight accommodation. At Spier, one can even enjoy opera, theatre and musical performances at their open-air amphitheatre.

For those who like to travel in style, South Africa is also an attractive destination. Today, most luxury liners are opting to avoid the Suez Canal because of ongoing troubles in the Middle East. South Africa is seen as a safe port of call, and more and more of these exclusive floating hotels are stopping here. In the first six months of 2002, 42 cruise liners docked in Cape Town, compared with a previous average of thirteen per year. Their passengers are particularly big spenders, some of them spending as much as R30 000 a day while in port.

There is also the opportunity to travel from Cape Town up through Africa on the prestigious Rovos Rail luxury train, including a stop at one of the Seven Natural Wonders of the World, Victoria Falls.

For those wanting luxury accommodation that doesn't rock them to sleep, South Africa offers some of the best hotels in the world and many, such as the Cape Grace, the Mount Nelson Hotel, Singita Private Game Lodge, and Sabi Sabi's fabulous Earth Lodge, are recipients of prestigious international awards.

Getting down to grassroots

For those wanting a more raw urban experience of Africa, the Soweto Shebeen Route has been launched by thirteen major shebeeners, the most well known of whom is Wandile Ndala. Ever since his township restaurant, called Wandie's, was awarded Best Restaurant (Ambience) status by the British publication *Winners' Dinners*, the rich and famous have been drawn to this humble dwelling, just down the road from Nelson Mandela and Desmond Tutu's homes. Inside, the walls are papered with the cards of day-trippers and business people from around the world, together with photos of Wandie with Evander Holyfield, Walter Sisulu, Jesse Jackson, Quincy Jones and Richard Branson.

South Africa is one of only five countries given 'approved destination' status by the Chinese government to Chinese tourists.

Township tours mushroomed after 1994, with a more recent positive development being the emergence of township B&Bs, like Vicky Ntozini's B&B in Khayelitsha, Cape Town's largest township. Vicky's B&B is sandwiched between ordinary township shacks, in a side alley, in what is called Site C. There are no signs or fancy neon lights to show the way, and the house is nothing more than a well-extended shack of corrugated iron and wood. This is a taste of real life in Khayelitsha, where nothing has been glossed over to dazzle the guests. Most visitors get to know about the place by word of mouth, and the guest book is full of names of international visitors.

At just 38 years old, Thabiso Tlelai is another of South Africa's new-generation leaders in the leisure and tourism industry. His passionate faith in South Africa's hotel industry fuelled the remarkable turnaround of the Don Group of executive suites that he took over in 1998. Tlelai ascertains that the country's hotels are among the most affordable in the world and our tourism package and its ancillaries are up with the best in the world. Says Tlelai, 'We have the weather, we have the facilities, we have the destinations.'

Let the games begin!

South Africans are a sports-mad nation. As a result, we have developed world-class stadiums, golf courses and athletes' facilities and we have also successfully hosted massive sporting spectaculars: the Rugby World Cup in 1995 and the African Cup of Nations Soccer in 1996. The Cricket World Cup will also take place in South Africa in 2003. These mega-events always bring not only good international exposure for South Africa, but also a great deal of foreign spending by sports fans, both during the event and afterwards, as they take time to visit the country or return to do so later.

Other events which showcase our organisational abilities are the Comrades Marathon between Durban and Pietermaritzburg, and the 105 km annual Cape Argus Pick 'n Pay Cycle Tour. The latter began with 500 riders in 1978 and today attracts 35 000 cyclists of all shapes, sizes and degrees of seriousness. Each cyclist receives a computer chip that records their individual time, making this the biggest cycle race of its kind in the world. The Tour earns Cape Town approximately R125 million each year, with more than 65 000 people visiting the Western Cape over the period of the race. Charities also benefit from the race, with over R2 million being ploughed back into the community and sports development.

We have also developed skills and experience in the bidding process for even bigger international events, like the Olympics and the Soccer World Cup, which we haven't been awarded – yet. Having failed before, we are in a position to learn from our mistakes and possibly make successful bids next time. The world has been assured that the 2010 Soccer World Cup will be held in Africa, which bodes well for South Africa's chances. And Cape Town is already considering bidding for the 2012 Summer Olympics.

It isn't only the big events that bring large numbers of tourists to our shores. Golfing tours already attract significant numbers of international travellers who come here specifically to play at our world-class, spectacular golf courses at extremely-competitive prices. The success of our own pro-golfers on the international circuit has also helped to promote South Africa's Sunshine Tour, which comprises eight tournaments, including venues in Zimbabwe, Sun City, the Wild Coast and the Cape. South Africa is well-positioned to continue to take advantage of this booming sports-tourism industry.

Parades in pinstripes

Sports fans are not the only large gatherings that we are hosting; there are the serious business-types too. Between 1999 and 2000, South Africa moved up a notch to twentieth on the world top-convention rating, according to the International Congress and Convention Association. Five years ago, South Africa wasn't even on the radar screen as a conference destination.

High profile events like the UN Conference on Racism, the international HIV/AIDS Convention and the inaugural meeting of the African Union in Durban, as well as the UN's World Summit on Sustainable Development in Johannesburg, have all helped to put South Africa on the map. The World Summit alone, which drew an estimated 23 000 people to Johannesburg from the UN's 189 member countries, is estimated to have generated R8 billion for the local economy, including more than 14 000 jobs. According to Trade and Industry Minister, Alec Erwin, quoted in *The Star* newspaper, 'The summit is a testimony to the self-confidence of our new democracy. This was apparently the largest United Nations summit that has been held. It must surely be the sense of being in a special place at a special time that allowed South Africa to be so bold.' He continues, 'I sensed another less visible outcome for South Africa of the WSSD. It was a decisive break with the paradigm that sees developing countries – in our case South Africa – as somehow subordinated to the developed when it comes to international relations.'

'The logistics of this event were immense. I still have to pinch myself to believe we actually did it. We were South Africans as capable as the best in the world.'

Alec Erwin, Minister of Trade & Industry, commenting on the WSSD

South African Tourism CEO Cheryl Carolus believes South Africa is perfectly poised for further growth in this highly-lucrative MICE – that's Meetings, Incentives, Conferences and Exhibitions – industry; an international tourism market worth in excess of $100 billion. The country has 1 700 conference venues, ranging from large city-based to remote *bosberaad*-type venues in spectacular mountain, coastal or bushveld settings. At the upper end of the market, following on the successes of the Sandton Convention Centre and Durban's International Convention Centre, Cape Town is about to launch the country's third state-of-the-art mega-facility which will be able to handle in excess of 5 000 delegates at one time. The exhibition space will rival the best in the world, with 10 000 square metres of pillar-free space.

According to a report released by Grant Thornton Kessel Feinstein, the entire MICE industry in South Africa contributes 246 000 jobs and R6 billion in salaries annually. Importantly, a study carried out by South African Tourism showed that ninety per cent of all delegates surveyed said they would return to South Africa, this time with their friends and family in tow.

Surfing the tidal wave

The tide seems to be turning in our favour as far as tourism is concerned. The rand is competitive, South Africa is seen increasingly as a safe destination in comparison to the USA, the Middle East and the Indian subcontinent, and the country offers foreign visitors an unforgettable experience. Tourists, particularly from Europe, are realising this more and more, and are arriving in unprecedented numbers. In total contrast to other destinations like Egypt, which saw a forty per cent drop in tourism after 11 September 2001, South Africa has had massive increases month-on-month. Tourist arrivals from the UK, South Africa's primary source market, increased 19.4 per cent in the first seven months of 2002, translating into a hundred extra jumbo jets full of people compared to the same period the year before. The 2002/3 holiday season, which normally starts in October, started early as a result of the UN World Summit, and is expected to be another bumper season thanks to the Cricket World Cup in March 2003. It helps too that in November 2002, Cape Town was voted fifth in a poll of the 'Fifty places to see before you die' by 20 000 viewers of the BBC programme *Holiday*. It was beaten only by the Grand Canyon, the Great Barrier Reef, Disney World and New Zealand's South Island. At the same time, 30 000 readers of the US *Condé Nast Traveler* magazine rated four South African hotels in the Top 25 in the world. Their UK readers placed South Africa tenth overall in the world as a preferred travel destination and gave the country first place for value-for-money.

World Trade Organisation rankings show that South Africa has moved up from 52nd most popular tourist destination in the early 1990s, to 25th today.

Far from being a one-hit wonder, this growth is expected to go from strength-to-strength, with new tourists coming from all over the world. For example, in November 2002, South Africa signed an agreement with China, in terms of which it will become only the fifth country in the world to be given 'approved destination' status for Chinese tourists. South African Tourism is not resting on its laurels however. It is working hard to ensure that we can attract even more foreign accents (and currencies) by profiling and targeting potential visitors in all regions of the world. This includes North America, which is still a largely-untapped market.

More and more South Africans are seeing what a gold mine tourism represents, and both government and business are rapidly putting the necessary into place to welcome this influx. Johannesburg International Airport has recently undergone a R1.9-billion facelift in anticipation of increasing the eleven million people that currently pass through it each year, to seventeen million by 2010. Airlines have recognised the need to increase the number of flights to South Africa. Lufthansa, for example, is increasing its weekly flights from seven to thirteen between October 2002 and March 2003, and they expect to increase their 350 000 passengers in 2002 to 450 000 in 2003.

Responding to this rising demand, classy hotels and homely B&Bs are springing up like mushrooms after the rain. The Department of Environmental Affairs & Tourism is helping individuals to become established in the industry, through initiatives such as a tourism handbook for small businesses. We each have our role to play. As the South African Tourism advertisement says, 'Smile and welcome foreigners to our beautiful country, let them know that we believe in our future and invite them to spread the word amongst their friends and family, and to return soon.'

7 Deep roots, diverse fruits

Cultivating radicals

'It's the rich, abrasive contact between different cultures rubbing up against each other that spreads all sorts of creative sparks.' These words, spoken by South African playwright and poet, Athol Fugard, capture the essence of one of our greatest strengths as a country. We are a nation of diverse cultures and, consequently, infinite possibilities for innovation and artistic expression.

Our cultures are like the roots of our nation. Roots are what connect us to our source, our identity, our sense of values, and to be deeply conscious of these things makes us 'radical'. Without roots, we would be blown over every time the gales of tragedy, pessimism or change gust across our personal or national horizon. Roots remind us that our true strength is within.

South Africa holds the Guinness Record for the tree with the deepest root in the world. A wild fig tree near Ohrigstad has a root that is 120 metres long.

South Africa's multilingual population is the fertile soil in which our cultural diversity is anchored. Each of our eleven official languages and the various minority languages spoken in this country add yet another ingredient to the land of our collective being. For each of us, our mother tongue is the language of our hearts, and our hearts are the source of all our best characteristics – like creativity, understanding and compassion. This places an obligation on us to learn to understand, respect and honour the diversity of languages in South Africa, an area in which we can undoubtedly improve. Indeed, can you name all eleven official languages? Try it now, for fun; the answer is at the end of this chapter.

If our cultural roots are strong, this country will bear delicious, succulent fruits in every area of human expression. The key to a bountiful harvest is how the farmer responds to Nature's moody ways, learning to work with Nature, rather than fight its elements. Similarly, we respond to our evolving cultural fusion and discover the kernel of inspiration that will reseed itself for the next generation.

This chapter is a celebration of all the fruits that are ripe for plucking in South Africa. Our boughs are already heavy with culturally-flavoured expressions in the arts. The rich soil of our nation is producing bumper crops of remarkable storytellers, actors, dancers, musicians, designers, artists and festivals. In fact, the harvest is so plentiful that we cannot possibly do justice to all of South Africa's icons of art and culture. Hence, we're sure you will forgive us if we happen to miss mentioning one or more of your own particular favourites.

Indaba, my children

Perhaps it is not surprising that we have such talented storytellers in South Africa, given the legacy of oral tradition in African culture, safeguarded by *sangomas* over countless generations. *Sangomas* play a multitude of roles in the spiritual life of African communities – healer, diviner, spiritual advisor, safeguard of beliefs and rituals, keeper of ancient wisdom and master storyteller. One of South Africa's better-known *sangomas* is the larger-than-life figure of Credo Vusamazulu Mutwa, whose wealth of knowledge spills over in his numerous books on African tradition, like *Indaba My Children, Isilwane* and *Song of the Stars*. Mutwa explains that 'these are the stories that old men and old women tell to boys and girls seated with open mouths around the spark-wreathed fires in the centres of the villages in the dark forests and on the aloe-scented plains of Africa. It is these stories that shaped Africa as we know it – years and years ago.' The contribution of these master storytellers is immense. Author Luisah Teish, who wrote the foreword to *Song of the Stars*, says, 'There is medicine for the soul here ... One feels his wonderful humanity and the genius of his people in these stories.'

We also have *sangomas* who are bringing their wisdom into the high-tech 21st century – people like Moses Dludlu who, since being initiated into the sacred profession, has become known as Shado. The décor and medicine that fills his consultation room in Barberton are all the paraphernalia that one associates with traditional doctors – masks, ceremonial drums, bowls of bark, roots and fronds, calabashes of beer, reed mats and animal skins. But there is also a computer whirring away in the background. Shado explains that the combination of traditional healing and modern technology is not contradictory, because by embracing technology we can remind people that whatever their circumstances may be, they don't have to abandon who they are. 'Through the Internet,' he says, 'I teach people how they can integrate their new circumstances with African systems and values. For example, today's story is about setting realistic goals. A weaver does not build a nest in a day and its mate does not lay its eggs until the nest is complete. These birds instinctively understand the natural way – a way in which shortcuts to creating the ideal situation can only spell disaster. It's all about patience, balance and harmony – simple things that, in the rush of the city, are easy to forget.'

Mother of books

Another modern storyteller of our soil is Gcina Mhlope, our very own *Nozincwadi*, which means 'Mother of Books'. This is in fact the name of her great aunt, who treasured words so much that she used to collect bits and pieces of paper with writing on them and store them in a big suitcase, despite the fact that she was illiterate. Inspired by this story and her own love of reading and writing, Mhlope has overcome formidable odds to become one of our foremost storytellers across a variety of media, from books, radio and plays, to videos and CDs. There is no doubt that her talent is world-class, having been translated into six languages (including German, French, Italian and Japanese), and winning numerous awards – like a Fringe First at the Edinburgh Festival, an Obbie in New York and a BBC Africa Service award for radio drama. She has also received honorary doctorates from London's Open University and the University of Natal. One of her favourite productions, called *Africa at the Opera*, was staged in Europe's opera houses with Ladysmith Black Mambazo. Perhaps the name she has given her daughter – Ikhwezi, which means 'Morning Star' – describes Mhlope as well. Certainly, it is a fitting symbol, for she truly gives hope for the dawning of a new day for African storytelling. As she puts it in the closing poem of her book, *Love Child*: 'The woman of Africa wants to sing a song of love. To bring back old wisdoms that will shine a new light. Brighter than the stars in the night sky.'

Another shining light is our winner of the 1991 Nobel Prize for Literature, Nadine Gordimer. The Nobel Committee praised her as someone 'who through her magnificent epic writing has – in the words of Alfred Nobel – been of very great benefit to humanity.' And then there is Cape Town-based JM Coetzee, only one of two writers in the world to have been awarded the Booker Prize for Fiction twice, in 1983 for *The Life and Times of Michael K*, and in 1999 for *Disgrace*. Zakes Mda, winner fo the Commonwealth Writers Prize, is also blazing a trail.

These are a few among many great writers who have animated the soul of South Africa with their living words. There are numerous others including CJ Langenhoven, Alan Paton, Solomon Plaatje, Lourens van der Post, Daleen Mathee, Wilbur Smith, Andre Brink, Herman Charles Bosman and Breyten Breytenbach. We rely on these great wordsmiths to echo back to us and to the world, the experiences of South Africa and its people. They allow us to look in the proverbial mirror and to laugh or cry at what we see in our own nation's reflection.

Larger than life

In the modern, storytelling medium of film, we're quick to point out how Australian and European stars have cracked the Hollywood scene. However, lest we forget, we have our very own glamour girl of the silver screen. Charlize Theron has gone from 'zero to hero' in the space of a few short years and is now one of the hottest stars in film. She has made eighteen films in eight years, playing alongside illustrious stars like Al Pacino, Johnny Depp, Keanu Reeves, Michael Caine, Robert de Niro, Robert Redford, Will Smith and Woody Allen, to name just a few. It's a fairytale, Cinderella-like story that took Theron from Benoni near Johannesburg to ballet school in New York, and on to a short modelling stint, before a Hollywood talent-scout spotted her throwing a tantrum in a bank. The rest, as they say, is history ... still in the making. Despite having adopted an American accent, which she claims was necessary to have a chance in professional acting in the USA, she remains an ambassador for South Africa.

Computicket, the online-entertainment booking system, now used all over the world, was created in South Africa.

On the other end of the media-celebrity spectrum, we have Durban-born Lara Logan, who is one of a string of South African journalists that have proved their metal in the tough world of global-news reporting. Working for GMTV, the largest breakfast show in the UK, she was the only journalist for a British-network on the frontline during the 2002 war in Afghanistan, bivouacked with Northern Alliance commander, General Babajan, at his rebel stronghold on the outskirts of Kabul. Lara's journey is typical of the grit and tenacity that South Africans are renowned for. She is also challenging the conventional wisdom about what it takes to survive in the brutal world of macho-journalism and in the face of human tragedy: 'I let it affect me. If I need to cry, I cry. I cope by embracing it, not suppressing it.'

Closer to home, one cannot mention television personalities without Felicia Mabuza-Suttle's name coming up. Not everybody likes TV talk-show host Felicia's style, but there's no question about her influence, her success, or her commitment. Born in South Africa, Felicia left for America to pursue a career in journalism and broadcast communication. She certainly made her mark, from being a university lecturer and marketing director for two Fortune 500 companies, to becoming director of marketing communications for the City of Atlanta. 'Making it in America is huge,' she reflects, 'but there is nothing more rewarding than making a difference at home.' She goes on to quote Dr Martin Luther King Jr as saying, 'An individual has not started living until he can live above his narrow concerns to the greater concerns of humanity.' And this is what her life's purpose is now – using the broadcast media 'for the betterment of one life at a time.'

Once again, there are numerous other media personalities to mention, like actor Jonathan Rands, of *Jock of the Bushveld* fame; Henry Cele of *Shaka Zulu;* Arnold Vosloo, the 'bad guy' in the Hollywood blockbuster *The Mummy*; talented news presenter, Khanyi Dlomo-Mkhize; investigative journalist and *Carte Blanche* co-host, Ruda Landman; tireless builders of South African pride like Dali Tambo, with his *People of the South* biographical talk show, and Denis Beckett with *Beckett's Trek*. No doubt, you have your favourites too.

Staging a comeback

More so than our success on the big (or small) silver screen, South Africa seems to have found its artistic niche in the production of stage theatre, with internationally acclaimed writer/directors like Athol Fugard among the luminaries that we can call our own. South Africa's unique blend of ancient and modern, traditional and contemporary, ethnic and cosmopolitan, make for an explosive concoction of creativity,

Athol Fugard is the second-most performed playwright in English in the world, after Shakespeare.

described by some as Afro-fusion. South African dance-choreographers seem to have a special ability to explore cross-cultural themes, socio-political ideas and timeless spiritual truths in ways both vivid and dynamic. The production of distinctively South African-flavoured musical shows that wow audiences on Broadway and the West End alike, are becoming the norm rather than the exception. Just think of the runaway successes of *Ipi Ntombi*, *District Six* and *Sarafina*, and more recent creations like the Soweto musical *Gumboots* and Richard

Loring's *African Footprint*. A musical that made waves in 2001 was *The Spear is Born: Bayede Shaka*, described as a South African King Arthur story, with Shaka's magic spear embodying powers similar to the mighty sword Excalibur in English mythology. Our cultural heritage is a treasure chest of inspiration for these sorts of productions.

District Six, David Kramer and Taliep Petersen's hit musical, ran to full houses for eighteen months in South Africa before going on tour overseas. Now, years later in 2002, it's making a comeback. For the coloured community, the musical was a breakthrough experience, one that helped to revive some of the tremendous creativity and pride that has always existed in their community. Let us not forget our 'Kaapse Klopse', who parade in a blaze of colour and sound through the streets of Cape Town every New Year's Day, commemorating the abolition of slavery, in our very own local version of the Rio Carnival. David Kramer also recently directed the latest production of one of today's hottest stage and television comedy-actors, Marc Lottering. *Big Stakes and Slap Chips* deals with the gambling phenomenon that has taken South Africa by storm in the past few years. The show is being taken abroad to Australia, Canada, New Zealand and the UK. Even before the success of *District Six* and its sequel, *Fairyland*, Kramer was a musical icon in South Africa, capturing the lives of ordinary,

South African musician, Lebo M, co-created the music for Disney's *The Lion King* with Sir Elton John and Sir Tim Rice. South African actor, Sello Maake ka Ncube, is currently playing Mafusa in the London production of the musical.

mostly rural, Afrikaans people. His unique style, replete with his trademark red *veldskoene*, has become known as *Blik*, perhaps a testimony to his no-frills, tell-it-like-it-is, grassroots approach to South Africa's indigenous rhythms. In one of his more recent artistic ventures, *Karoo Kitaar Blues*, Kramer brought together the eclectic and eccentric talents of musicians from the most far-flung, remote corners of the country, to put their extraordinary talents under the city spotlight.

Fellow music maestro, Todd Twala, claims that 'there is more untapped potential in townships like Johannesburg's Soweto and Phameng outside Bloemfontein, than anywhere else on Earth.' He speaks from experience, as creator and producer of the South African musical *Umoja*, which is packing houses from London and Sydney to Lagos and Amsterdam. 'This is the golden age for our young talent. They are carrying the flag for African musicals with the same spirit as our athletes competing in the Olympic Games and the World Cup soccer.' Cynda Eatock, a veteran of Broadway shows in the 1980s and today a talent scout, echoes these sentiments. 'It's an exciting time – TV and pop music now offer as much opportunity as stage musical roles ... Our hottest stage hits right now are still the 'skins and feathers' traditional musicals, but it's changing fast. My biggest classes now are for hip-hop music, and I'm helping R&B stars produce slick music videos for their record hits.'

Voices of freedom

Many of the musical successes of today take their inspiration from the successful solo or group artists that have stepped out of the shadows of apartheid South Africa into the spotlight of international success. Miriam Makeba is the original diva in this respect. She is one of those timeless icons of the South African soil, a diamond that has sparkled and dazzled on the world stage and yet remains woefully undervalued in this, her home country. Makeba's breakthrough came with starring roles in the musical *King Kong* and the documentary, *Come Back Africa*. In 1967, she won a Grammy Award for *An Evening With Belafonte/Makeba*, making her the first African recording artist in the world to be awarded this prestigious prize. In 1987, she was invited to join Paul Simon on his world *Graceland* tour and more than a decade later, was still performing to packed audiences at London's Royal Festival Hall and Paris's Olympia Theatre. And the accolades continue to pile up. Makeba's 2000 album, *Homeland*, which celebrated her return to South Africa after a thirty-year exile, was nominated for a Grammy Award in the World Music Category. Beyond the musical sphere, Makeba's impact is no less inspiring. In her tireless support for the civil-rights movement, she has twice addressed the United Nations General Assembly on the scourge of apartheid in South Africa and, in 1996, was awarded the Dag Hammerskjöld Peace Prize. How privileged we are to have her back home and may we never take this living legend for granted. As the *New York Times* reminds us, 'her voice evokes a land where song has a life-saving ability to lift the heart.'

Other South African music icons include the likes of Hugh Masekela, Abdullah Ibrahim, Johnny Clegg, Sipho 'Hotstix' Mabuse, Lucky Dube, the Soweto String Quartet, Mimi Coertse, Amampondo, PJ Powers, Mango Groove and Vusi Mahlasela. Mahlasela is typical of our more recent homegrown talent, for whom 'the world is but an oyster'. Weaned on guitars fashioned from cooking-oil tins and paraffin containers with fishing-line strings, he is today a truly-international artist: musician, poet, composer, songwriter and cultural activist.

In late 2002, Mahlasela clinched a deal with American label, ATO Records. The label was formed in 2000 and is part owned by Dave Matthews, the South African-born leader of The Dave Matthews Band, America's most successful contemporary music group. Mahlasela was a guest vocalist on the title track of the Dave Matthews Band album, *Everyday*. The album went on to debut at number one on the Billboard album charts in early 2001, and has so far sold over three million copies around the world. ATO also recently launched a film company, ATO Pictures, and will shortly release the soundtrack album to *Amandla! The Revolution In Four Part Harmony*, a documentary film which won two prestigious Sundance Film Festival awards in 2002. The film charts the crucial role of song during the apartheid struggle, with Vusi emerging as one of the film's stars.

**'In my African Dream, you touched my soul
Raised up the children, you made them whole.'**

**Johnny Clegg
from 'In my African Dream'**

What makes our artists, like Mahlasela, so globally compelling, is their powerful sense of meaning. For instance, Mahlasela dedicates his latest CD, *Miyela Afrika*, to 'the living spirit of the African Renaissance ... with full respect to the statement *Ngugi wa Thiongo*: 'Africa, teach your children the ancient songs that glorify the spirit of collective good."

This is art with a message and Mahlasela is not the exception. All of our artists have an ability to speak to the pressing needs of our time. Who can forget the haunting legacy of songs by Johnny Clegg and his Juluka partner Sipho Mchunu. Johnny Clegg has sung a remarkable anthology of our historical journey from injustice to freedom – from 'Third World Child', 'Orphans of An Empire' and 'Gunship Ghetto', to 'Asimbonanga', 'Kilimanjaro' and 'Tough Enough'. His celebration of African culture is also unforgettable, with 'Impi', 'Scatterlings of Africa' and 'Great Heart', now popular as anthems at our national sporting events. Not only do our musicians get our feet tapping; they get our hearts beating, our conscience sparking and our souls stretching as well.

Shaping our destiny

One of South Africa's unique contributions to the world must be its culturally-infused art. Did you know that the Oliewenhout Art Museum in Bloemfontein features an African Carousel, complete with Sotho mythological figures? Or that the Mapungubwe Exhibition includes an ancient gold rhino, bowl and sceptre, all part of the University of Pretoria's extensive collection? While we need to be careful not to put African people into stereotypical ethnic boxes or expect African art not to continue to evolve along with all the modern influences of Western development, the African cultural heritage is so rich and valuable that it is important to recall and to record the old ways for posterity. Generations to come will draw inspiration from the indigenous wisdom of Africa.

The internationally sought-after Ardmore ceramics are a good example of this, a product of cultural inheritance expressed through modern artistic design and driven by social upliftment. The Ardmore Ceramic Art Studio was established in the central Drakensberg region of KwaZulu-Natal by the unlikely duo of Fee Halsted-Berming and Bonakele Ntshalintshali. In the beginning, Fee, a Zimbabwean-born ceramist and painter, took on Bonakele, her domestic worker's daughter, as an apprentice. Soon, their individual strengths – Fee's extensive knowledge of meticulously-ordered ceramic sculptural form and Bonakele's exuberant, rhythmic reinterpretations of biblical narratives and traditional African rituals – were combining to create truly unique, wildly-imaginative items bursting with vivid colours and African images. The result is nothing ever seen before – teapots in the shape of blue elephants and turquoise warthogs, and Jonah being spat from the whale's mouth, or vases growing yellow-and-black zebras, multi-coloured guinea fowl and slithering snakes. Distributors like Charles Grieg Jewellers have recognised the work for its intrinsic value as well as for its passion and vision, capturing the soul and vibrancy of Africa. This has been borne out by the interest shown by some of the most discerning collectors of ceramics in the world.

Projects like Ardmore are essential to cultivating pride in South African creations and to challenging the unfortunately pervasive belief that all things from 'overseas' must be better. Our Christmas celebrations reflect the legacy of cultural imperialism. Why else would so many South Africans insist on sending cards and displaying decorations at Christmas time that recall images of snow and sleigh-bells? There was almost certainly no snow in Bethlehem in Israel when Jesus was born; neither is there snow in Africa during summer. But it is an example of how we have allowed popular culture to be influenced and dominated by the Western countries of the Northern Hemisphere. There are signs that the times are changing, however, through initiatives like the Christmas Africa project. The catalyst, four years ago, was the Liberty Foundation's Christmas Africa competition. This produced a wealth of new interpretations of the Christmas theme, using home-grown talents and materials. Today, Christmas Africa is an organisation which aims to create an awareness so strong, that to have imported Christmas decorations will soon be as inappropriate as wearing fur or buying ivory. Their products are refreshingly different – Christmas trees made of twirly galvanised wire, brilliantly-coloured Zulu ear ornaments to 'deck the halls', and beaded Zulu-doll angels, to mention but a few. Now, not only is Christmas taking on a new look, but it is providing much-needed employment. For some 400 women living in the remote rural areas of northern KwaZulu-Natal, the Africanisation of Christmas has brought a noticeable improvement in their quality of life. Beaders Veronica Zikhali and her daughter Jabu, for example, have managed to quadruple their meagre monthly earnings from R500 to R2 000. Why support someone else's people, when we can support our own, especially at Christmas?

Doing it in style

One of the central themes of this book is pride – in who we are, where we come from and what makes us unique. Hence we salute Barbara Tyrrell, for whom recording the 'old ways' has been a life work and an enduring legacy. Tyrrell first took to the open road and dusty bushveld in 1944 – one woman, alone in a campervan, seeking to understand the colourful tapestry of southern Africa's indigenous people, and to honour it with artwork. She learnt about the importance of their manners, customs and beliefs, and how it was expressed in their dress. She realised, for example, that in Zulu culture, beadwork tells the life story of a person. Later, she learnt that each tribe's custom is different and that one's status is indicated by the manner of dress. Thus began a monumental study of tribal dress and regalia and its significance. Over a fifty-year period, she completed more than a thousand pictures, many of them featured in her books, *The Tribal Peoples of Southern Africa* and *African Heritage*. These art collections, and numerous others like it, are a powerful reminder of the amazing inheritance of cultural inspiration that we have in South Africa.

Events like the Face of Africa competition continue to celebrate this theme. They not only show off the stunning beauty of African people, but give a boost to the whole fashion industry, from clothing and beauty products, to jewellery and accessories. In 2001, for example, the Face of Africa was an opportunity to showcase the best of South Africa's gold jewellery, by linking it with the Riches of Africa competition. Competitions like these add momentum to the initial impetus created by South African beauty celebrities of yesteryear, like Penny Coelen-Rey, Anneline Kriel (also the 1974 Miss World) and Robyn Poole. There is now a whole new generation of South African models making it big. Nicola Breytenbach, for instance, has just stepped into the shoes of Revlon's former supermodel, Cindy Crawford, along with three other 'chosen ones' from across the globe. She joins a prestigious list of Revlon faces which include Melanie Griffith, Cybill Shepherd and, more recently, Shania Twain and Halle Berry. Similarly, South African Khanyi Dhlomo-Mkhize has joined the Lux stable of international beauty stars, following in the footsteps of former Lux faces from South Africa, Robyn Poole and Felicia Mabuza-Suttle. Clearly, these glamorous images do not represent the *only* face of South Africa, but it is good to know that we can compete with the best in the world in all aspects of life.

Fashion competitions and branded beauties like these are just the 'ears of the hippopotamus' (to use the African equivalent expression of 'the tip of the iceberg') – they are symptomatic of a much deeper revolution taking place: the Afro-chic fashion trend we mentioned earlier in the book. Shakur Olla, who was born and bred in that melting pot of cultural fusion that used to be Cape Town's District Six, is living proof of, in his own words, 'a renaissance in African fashion [providing] a sophisticated, modern alternative to the craft theme usually associated with African fashion.' From humble beginnings working in the clothing and textile industry, Shakur left South Africa in 1979 to work in the USA, only to return in 1985 and found United Textiles. In 1994 he founded Shakur Olla Design and created Incasa (Xhosa for 'good taste'), his African signature line. By 1999, he had opened his lifestyle flagship store in Green Point, Cape Town, and quickly became the fastest-selling label in South Africa, earning him the *Fair Lady* Best Brand Award in 2000. Not only is his range selling alongside prominent international labels, he has managed to *outsell* them all. His recipe for success, which could well have been the title for this book, or a motto for the new South Africa, is 'world style with an African edge.'

Another innovative fashion pioneer with a South African feel is Hooked on Hemp SA Ltd, an empowerment company focussing on developing enterprises in various production activities relating to industrial hemp as a textile. This label's design philosophy is to produce clothes that are durable, of good quality and created as 'Afro-expressions', not fashion.

Being a good sport

One thing that is highly fashionable in South Africa, and which we know how to celebrate (and curse), is sport. We can't deny it – South Africa is a sports-besotted nation! Apart from the roller-coaster fortunes of our national sports sides, South Africa has an undeniable knack for producing some remarkable, world-beating, individual athletes of whom we can be exceptionally proud. Since the days when our brilliant, barefooted *boere-meisie*, Zola Budd, who caused such a stir in the international athletics arena, we have had plenty to cheer about. Elana Meyer, Hezekiel Sepeng, Llewellyn Herbert, Hestrie Cloete, Penny Heyns and Terence Parkin are just some of the many world champions and Olympic medallists that have blazed a trail as supreme athletes. There is the incredible story of true South African grit in the form of Natalie du Toit, who lost her left leg above the knee in a car accident in February 2001 and went on to win two swimming gold medals and

The Eastern Cape has produced more boxing world champions than any comparable region of any other country.

break two world records at the 2002 Commonwealth Games in Manchester. We have excelled in other individual sports as well. In tennis, Amanda Coetzer and Wayne Ferreira have both enjoyed Top 10 rankings, while in golf, 'The Big Easy' (Ernie Els) and 'The Golden Goose' (Retief Goosen) have followed in the legendary footsteps of past master, Gary Player. With talents like 'Baby Jake' Matlala and numerous others, we have also dominated the boxing rings of the world.

Fun and laughter

Beyond the blood, sweat and tears of sports, we also have a genius for comedy. 'You have to laugh, or else you cry,' sings Clare Johnston, lead singer of the South African band, Mango Groove. What a truism, in a country where we have such a bittersweet history, such a culturally-diverse population and such enormous social challenges to face and overcome. Fortunately, South Africans are becoming quite good at laughing at themselves, especially since the veil has lifted on our most-recent shadowy past. Although, even in those days, we had brave satirists like Jeremy Taylor and Pieter Dirk-Uys, the latter with his legendary white-Afrikaner caricature, Evita Bezuidenhout. More recently, the likes of Marc Lottering, with his alter-ego, Aunty Merle, have taken centre-stage. Then, there are our politically- and culturally-insightful cartoonists, like Zapiro and the creators of the hilarious *Madam and Eve* strip. Ten years since the launch of *Madam and Eve* in 1992, its trio of creators – Stephen Francis, Harry Dugmore and Rico Schacherl – are still going strong, with their lovable characters coming to life in a television series of the same name. Their collections, like *All Aboard the Gravy Train* and *Somewhere Over the Rainbow Nation*, are almost instant bestsellers – although life in South Africa certainly presents them with plenty of source material!

It is also a positive sign that we are learning to celebrate our diversity of artistic talent by way of a growing number of festivals. Best known are the Standard Bank National Arts Festival in Grahamstown, the Klein Karoo Nationale Kunsfees (KKNK) in Oudtshoorn, the Knysna Oyster Festival and the Hermanus Whale Festival. With the Grahamstown Festival as the mecca for English art and culture, the KKNK, a relatively new kid on the festival block, is a celebration of our Afrikaans talent. In 2002, it attracted roughly 30 000 people every day, with ticket sales of 164 000 for performances over the two-week period, including 89 shows of 186 productions that varied daily. In Knysna, around nine million oysters are cultivated for the Oyster Festival in July each year, while one of the most scenic marathons in the world is run against a breathtaking backdrop of mountains, lakes, lagoons and forests.

If music is what you're after, then you are even more spoilt for choice. There is the North Sea Jazz Festival at the Good Hope Centre in Cape Town; the WOMAD (World Music Arts & Dance) Festival at Benoni's Bluegum Creek; the Rustler's Valley Easter Festival for New-Age types; the Splashy Fen Festival in the southern Drakensberg; the Woodstock Festival at Heidelberg; the Up the Creek Festival on the Breede River outside Swellendam; and the Oppikoppie Festival for 'artists who are pushing the edges of their art'. In South Africa, we will find almost any excuse for a fun time. We even have festivals in honour of potatoes (Napier), cherries (Ficksberg), and cheese and wine (Bonnievale); in fact, just about anything that grows. If current trends continue, we will become the Festival Nation of the World, and why not! We have so much to celebrate.

The answer to the question at the beginning of the chapter – South Africa's eleven official languages are, in alphabetical order, Afrikaans, English, IsiXhosa, IsiZulu, Ndebele, Sepedi, Sesotho, Setswana, Siswati, Tshivenda and Xitsonga.

8 Timeless icons

Historians of the future will not only be fascinated by South Africa's fascist/apartheid experiment, but will also be intrigued and respectful of the remarkable lives of numerous legendary personalities that were forged in the fires of this country. Some, like the mercurial Shaka and Paul Kruger, were larger-than-life symbols of unity and strength for the proud cultures of this diverse land. Others like Cecil Rhodes and Harry Oppenheimer, were ambitious, yet visionary business magnates, who helped to turn South Africa's assets into wealth. And still others, like Steve Biko and Helen Suzman, became the voice of the voiceless in our nation's struggle for freedom and dignity.

However, standing out above even these are several leaders who have left a positive and lasting legacy of hope and peace for the entire world. Living in South Africa today, we tend to take these political, philosophical and moral giants for granted. We fail to fully comprehend that the world will be guided and inspired by their ideas and values for generations to come. In this chapter, we pay fleeting tribute to six of these timeless icons, namely Mahatma Gandhi, Jan Smuts, Albert Luthuli, Desmond Tutu, FW de Klerk and Nelson Mandela.

Mahatma Gandhi

Mohandas Karamchand Gandhi – affectionately known by his honorary title 'Mahatma', which means 'Great Soul' – is one of those iconic individuals whose political and moral influence towers over the landscape of the twentieth century. His life was a powerful testimony to the revolutionary practice of peaceful resistance and to the spiritual philosophy of non-violence. Many of Gandhi's ideas, including his 'satyagraha' method (which means literally 'holding to the truth'), were first conceived and tested in South Africa, in the two decades he spent here after arriving as a newly-qualified lawyer in 1893.

In fact, in later years, Gandhi paid our country a great tribute by saying: 'My love for South Africa and my concern for her problems are no less than for India.' Recalling how his campaign of non-violent resistance to racial injustice began when he was thrown off a train in Pietermaritzburg for daring to sit in a first class coach, Gandhi said: 'I was afraid for my very life ... What was my duty, I asked myself. Should I go back to India, or should I go forward, with God as my helper, and face whatever was in store for me? I decided to stay and suffer. My active non-violence began from that date.'

Gandhi established the Natal Indian Congress in 1894. It was the first anti-colonial political organisation in the country, if not in the world. Gandhi's *satyagraha* campaign of defiance against the South African authorities began in earnest in 1907 and reached its climax in 1913 with a march by 5 000 indentured workers from the coal mines of Natal. It was during this time (in 1910) that Russian Count Leo Tolstoy wrote to him to say that his activity in the Transvaal 'is the most essential work now being done in the world, and in which ... all the world will undoubtedly take part.'

Gandhi's thinking and actions helped to shape the liberation struggle in South Africa, that continued for almost eighty years after his return to India in 1915. In fact, Gandhi and John Dube, first President of the African National Congress, were neighbours in Inanda, and each influenced the other. Both

'I was born in India but made in South Africa ... it was after I went to South Africa that I became what I am now.'

Mahatma Gandhi
On his work in South Africa

men, for instance, established monuments to human development at about the same time and within a stone's throw of each other: the Ohlange Institute and the Phoenix Settlement. Furthermore, both the African People's Organisation (APO) and the ANC, were established during Gandhi's most active period of political resistance in South Africa.

Summing up his life's mission, Gandhi once said, 'If we look into the future, is it not a heritage we have to leave to posterity, that all the different races co-mingle and produce a civilisation that perhaps the world has not yet seen?' And then, in 1939, almost prophetically, 'I am hoping that some day from among the youths born in South Africa, a person will rise who will stand up for the rights of his countrymen domiciled there, and make the vindication of those rights his life's mission.'

When Nelson Mandela became South Africa's first democratically-elected President, it was the realisation of Gandhi's hope for South Africa. As Mandela began his first term of office, he paid tribute in turn to the role that Gandhi had played in South Africa's emancipation and called on the nation to take up the challenging task of building the civilisation of which Gandhi had spoken: 'Gandhi's magnificent example of personal sacrifice and dedication in the face of oppression was one of his many legacies to our country and to the world. He showed us that it was necessary to brave imprisonment if truth and justice were to triumph over evil. The values of tolerance, mutual respect and unity for which he stood and acted, had a profound influence on our liberation movement, and on my own thinking. They inspire us today in our efforts of reconciliation and nation-building. That legacy extends to methods of struggle and mobilisation for social change. As our people were the agents of their own liberation, defying oppression and deprivation, they are now critical to the program of reconstruction and development, both as beneficiary and driving force.'

Mandela even went as far as to say that 'the Gandhian philosophy may be a key to human survival in the 21st century.' It is ironic that Gandhi, this grandfather of the peace movement, was never awarded the Nobel Peace Prize, despite being nominated in 1937, 1938, 1939, 1947 and, finally, a few days before he was murdered, in January 1948. Nevertheless, we can be proud that Gandhi's legacy lives on in the world, through his challenging ideas, his profound philosophies and, most visibly, through South Africa's successful transformation. The reciprocal influences of Gandhi on South Africa and vice versa are explored in more detail in the book *Gandhiji's Vision Of A Free South Africa: A Collection Of Articles*, compiled by ES Reddy.

Jan Smuts

Some may be surprised at the inclusion of Jan Christiaan Smuts, former Prime Minister of South Africa, as one of our timeless icons. His heavy-handed command-and-control political style was certainly not beyond reproach, as his clashes with Gandhi demonstrated on several occasions. Nevertheless, his political achievements, both in South Africa and on the international stage, should not be ignored. Also, lest we forget, it was only when he lost the 1948 election to the more conservative Nationalist Party, that the era of institutionalised apartheid truly began. In addition, it is his scientific and philosophical contribution that places him firmly in the league of twentieth-century personalities that left a lasting legacy.

As far as Smuts' political achievements are concerned, he was a soldier and statesman who was twice Prime Minister of South Africa (1919–1924 and 1939–1948). He fought in the Second South African War (1899–1902), but by 1904 concluded that the cooperation of Boer and British elements was essential to realise the true potential of South Africa. To this end, Smuts was instrumental in the creation of the Union of South Africa in 1910. Having gained international repute during World War I, he was appointed a member of the Imperial War Cabinet in London and helped draft the League of Nations covenant, which was the first attempt to create a multilateral organisation that would help secure world peace. Although he signed the Treaty of Versailles, he protested (prophetically) that its terms would outrage Germany and prevent the harmonious world order that he believed could best be served by the League of Nations. Smuts was also active in gathering support for Britain and leading South Africa's efforts in World War II, during which he became a trusted confidant of Winston Churchill. Following on from his work with the League of Nations, Smuts was charged with drafting the Preamble of the United Nations Charter, which was to succeed the League of Nations. It is worth quoting the text of the Preamble

'We the peoples of the United Nations determine ... to promote social progress and better standards of life in larger freedom ...'

Jan Smuts
From the United Nations Charter

here and remembering that these are largely the words of Smuts:

'We, the peoples of the United Nations, determine:
- to save succeeding generations from the scourge of war, which twice in our lifetime has brought untold sorrow to mankind, and
- to reaffirm faith in fundamental human rights, in the dignity and worth of the human person, in the equal rights of men and women and of nations large and small, and
- to establish conditions under which justice and respect for the obligations arising from treaties and other sources of international law can be maintained, and
- to promote social progress and better standards of life in larger freedom,

And for these ends:
- to practise tolerance and live together in peace with one another as good neighbours, and

- to unite our strength to maintain international peace and security, and
- to ensure, by the acceptance of principles and the institution of methods, that armed force shall not be used, save in the common interest, and
- to employ international machinery for the promotion of the economic and social advancement of all peoples,

Have resolved to combine our efforts to accomplish these aims.

Accordingly, our respective governments, through representatives assembled in the city of San Francisco, who have exhibited their full powers found to be in good and due form, have agreed to the present Charter of the United Nations and do hereby establish an international organisation to be known as the United Nations. (26 June 1945).'

Reflecting on the task of the United Nations, and reflecting his own broader vision for a better world order, Smuts had this to say: 'Without feeding on illusions, without nursing the impossible, there is yet much in the common life of the people which can be remedied, much unnecessary inequality and privilege to be levelled away, much common-sense opportunity to be erected as the common birthright and public atmosphere – for all to enjoy as a right. Health, housing, education, decent social amenities, provision against avoidable insecurities – all these simple goods and much more can be provided for all, and thus a common higher level of life be achieved for all. As between the nations, a new spirit of human solidarity can be cultivated, and economic conditions can be built up which will strike at the root causes of war, and thus lay deeper foundations for world peace. With honesty and sincerity on our part, it is possible to make basic reforms both for national and international life, which will give mankind a new chance of survival and of progress. Let this programme, by no means too ambitious, be our task, and let us now already, even in the midst of war, begin to prepare for it.'

In addition to his important political role in attempting to unify the whites of South Africa, and to lay the platform for a more stable and equitable post-war world, Smuts was a brilliant scholar who graduated in science, literature and law, and wrote the important scientific and philosophical treatise *Holism and Evolution* (1926). Synthesising Darwin's theory of evolution, Einstein's theory of relativity and his own thinking, Smuts coined the term 'holism' to describe how the driving force behind evolution is the formation of ever more complex and comprehensive integrations, or wholes. He cited considerable scientific evidence of this holistic principle at work, from the formation of inorganic chemical compounds, through various biological levels (plant, animal and human), to human personality and organisation within society.

In the preface to his book, Smuts said, 'It is my belief that holism and the holistic point of view will prove important in their bearings on some of the main problems of science and philosophy, ethics, art and allied subjects … [and] how it affects the higher spiritual interests of mankind.' This proved prophetic indeed, since the theory of holism described all the elements of what later became known as General Systems Theory, or systems thinking, which is applied today in disciplines ranging from astronomy, physics, biology and medicine, to economics, management, psychology and spirituality. In fact, an Internet search on 'holism' returns more than 30 000 sites, and 'holistic' more than 1.2 million. Hence, through the United Nations and his theory of holism, Smuts has left a legacy for the improvement of the lot of humankind.

Albert Luthuli

Unfortunately, while Jan Smuts did a great deal to mend fences between the Afrikaners and the English, and to work towards peace on an international level, he did not work hard enough towards promoting democracy for all South Africans. As a result, black, Asian and coloured people in South Africa still had to fight passionately for their basic rights. It was into this environment that Albert John Luthuli, the first South African to win the Nobel Peace Prize, was born in 1898, and was exposed to the racism and tribalism against which he was to spend the majority of his life fighting.

First and foremost, Albert Luthuli had a strong Christian belief in fairness, equality and dignity, and it was these beliefs that guided his thinking. Being a Christian did not mean that he was by definition a pacifist. He was more of the school that believed in forcing out the bad and replacing it with the good, as Jesus did when he threw the moneylenders out of the temple. He was a lay preacher for many years, and he became chairman of the South African Board of the Congregationalist Church of America, president of the Natal Mission Conference, and an executive member of the Christian Council of South Africa. In 1938 he was a delegate to the International Missionary Conference in Madras, India, and in 1948 he spent nine months on a lecture tour of the United States.

Luthuli followed a rule of 'sacrificial service', meaning that he was prepared to sacrifice his own comfort in the service of his people. This is precisely what he did when he gave up his job as a teacher at Adam's College in Natal in 1936, where he was one of only two black teachers, to become the democratically-elected chief of his 5 000-strong tribe, for a significantly lower salary. He held this position until 1952, when the apartheid government removed him from office by banning traditional leaders from being involved in politics. Chief Luthuli had become involved increasingly in the ANC since joining the organisation in 1945, after having been exposed more and more to the very real issues of landlessness and lack of basic rights for his people. He had been elected Provincial President of the organisation in Natal in 1951. Once deposed from his chieftainship by the government, he was elected to the position of President-General of the ANC in 1952.

Luthuli was almost immediately banned by the government and forced to restrict his movements to the Lower Tugela area. The ban was renewed continuously right up to his death in 1967. Despite these restrictions however, he was nonetheless arrested along with 155 other leaders of virtually every existing anti-apartheid movement in the country in 1956, and charged with high treason. The treason trial lasted for four years, until all the accused were found 'not guilty' in March 1961.

'I personally believe that here in South Africa, with all our diversities of colour and race, we will show the world a new pattern of democracy ... on the basis, not of colour, but of human values.'

Albert Luthuli
Speaking at his trial in 1958

In spite of the harassment to which he was personally subjected and the obvious injustices brought upon the majority of South Africans, Chief Luthuli never faltered in his belief that the ANC should not become a violent movement. While he said that anyone who thought he was a pacifist should try to steal his chickens, he believed that a policy of non-violent struggle against apartheid was more effective for gaining the support of most South Africans and the rest of the world, as well as averting a potential civil war in the country. It was this stance that earned him international recognition and the Nobel Peace Prize in 1960. The government allowed him a passport to travel to Oslo to accept the prize on condition that he did not get involved in any political campaigning. Nevertheless, his name still appeared on human rights petitions presented to the UN, the students of Glasgow University elected him as their Rector, the National Union of South African Students (NUSAS) made him their Honorary President, and he was nominated as President of the South African Colored People's Congress.

It was only later, when it became clear that the Nationalist Government did not see a problem with their apartheid policies and was therefore not interested in talking about a solution, that Luthuli accepted that some measure of targeted violence against state institutions, like army installations, was necessary. He believed, though, that this should be accomplished through a military movement separate from the ANC, which was ultimately the case when *Umkhonto we Sizwe* was established by Nelson Mandela.

Albert Luthuli was recognised as an intelligent and eloquent leader, with forward-thinking ideas and an unflinching commitment to non-racialism. He rejected the idea that democracy was impossible in a country as heterogeneous as South Africa. In a speech in Johannesburg during his trial in 1958, he said: 'I personally believe that here in South Africa, with all our diversities of colour and race, we will show the world a new pattern of democracy. I think there is a challenge to us in South Africa to set a new example for the world. We can build a homogenous South Africa on the basis not of colour but of human values.'

Let us never forget these words, and keep working towards a South Africa that fulfils the promise that Chief Albert Luthuli foresaw.

Desmond Tutu

Desmond Mpilo Tutu is one of those remarkable individuals, who is recognised in South Africa and by the world, as being one of the outstanding pragmatic visionaries of the twentieth century, a spiritual leader who has helped to regenerate the moral fibre of our modern society. Born in Klerksdorp and trained as a teacher, he went on to study for the ministry and become the first black Dean at the Anglican cathedral in Johannesburg in 1975. He was consecrated Bishop of Lesotho in 1976 and became General Secretary of the South African Council of Churches in 1978.

What distinguished Tutu, however, was not so much his rise through the ranks of the Anglican Church, but rather his uncompromising and vocal stand against apartheid. He constantly sought to be the voice of reason and warning in a highly-volatile political environment: 'I myself have said times without number that I am opposed to all forms of violence, that of those who wish to uphold the vicious and unjust and totally immoral and evil system of apartheid and of those who want to overthrow that system ... I have said many times before that this institutionalised structural violence of South Africa is making many blacks desperate as they despair of peaceful change, for until 1960, and since 1912, their political groups have struggled valiantly to bring about change by peaceful means. But what has been the result? A growing intransigence on the part of the authorities, replying with teargas, police dogs, police bullets and death; an escalating violence that has shut out the possibility of peaceful negotiation ... Many blacks have despaired of peaceful change. I have warned that when people become desperate, then they will use desperate methods.'

Not surprisingly, these views did not win him any favour with the reigning political leaders. In 1980, the government confiscated his passport in reprisal for his call for an international boycott of South African coal. Nevertheless, in 1984, he was awarded the Nobel Peace Prize in recognition of his non-violent anti-apartheid campaign. He proceeded to establish the Southern African Refugee Scholarship Fund with his prize money, enabling disadvantaged students to further their studies. Tutu's commitment to creating a free and democratic South Africa intensified as he became Bishop of Johannesburg in 1985, and Archbishop of Cape Town and head of the Anglican Church in Southern Africa in 1986.

When the first democratic elections eventually came about in 1994, he was elated and coined the now widely-used terms 'rainbow nation' and 'the rainbow people of God' to describe the new South Africa. At the same time, he was able to put the challenge that lay ahead into its proper perspective, saying: 'To build a nation we must do more than slip a ballot paper into a box. Black consciousness has not yet completed its work. We need to draw on its strengths and assert our self-worth, behaving as people who are confident in ourselves and in our nation. We need to recapture *ubuntu*, that gift Africans have for the world which says that a person can be a person only through other persons. If we recognise our own self-worth, we will respect the worth of others and have reverence for life.'

> **'We need to recapture *ubuntu*, that gift Africans have for the world which says that a person can be a person only through other persons.'**
>
> **Archibishop Desmond Tutu**

After retiring as Archbishop in 1996, Tutu became Chairperson of the Truth and Reconciliation Commission in South Africa, and presided over the traumatic revelation of the political crimes against humanity committed during the apartheid era. The image of him weeping with grief and emotional exhaustion during the hearings is a haunting reminder of the horrors that this country and its people have witnessed. Explaining the value of the TRC, he expressed the hope that 'by opening wounds to cleanse them, the TRC will thereby stop them from festering. We cannot be facile and say bygones will be bygones, because they will not be bygones and will return to haunt us. True reconciliation is never cheap, for it is based on forgiveness which is costly. Forgiveness in turn depends on repentance, which has to be based on an acknowledgement of what was done wrong, and therefore on disclosure of the truth. You cannot forgive what you do not know.'

A steady flow of tributes to Tutu, including honorary degrees and prizes, pour in annually and will no doubt continue to do so. Former US President Bill Clinton praised Tutu as 'a leader in both struggle and reconciliation [who] reminds us that the search for justice begins in the heart,' while Mandela said that Tutu's voice will always be the voice of the voiceless. US Reverend David du Plantier from Ohio reflected that 'no other living Anglican has so captured the imagination of the world and set hearts on fire, with his intense faith, acute wit and powerful manifestation of God's love.' Compilations of his sermons, speeches and reflections, like *No Future Without Forgiveness* and *The Rainbow People of God*, are a source of deep inspiration and considerable wisdom. Through his positive yet pragmatic spirit, Tutu is a living symbol of the hopes and prayers of many in the world, showing that it is indeed possible to move beyond hatred and revenge to forgiveness and celebration of our common humanity.

FW de Klerk

FW de Klerk was born into a political family. His father was a cabinet minister, his uncle, Hans Strijdom, was Prime Minister, and his brother, Willem, a liberal newspaperman and one of the founders of the Democratic Party. De Klerk entered politics himself as the National Party MP for Vereeniging in 1972, turning down an offer of a professorship in administrative law at Potchefstroom University (where he had earlier achieved an LLB degree cum laude).

With a long history in the National Party, De Klerk was not publicly known for advocating reform. He had served as a minister in various portfolios under John Vorster and PW Botha, and while serving as Minister of National Education and Planning from 1984 to 1989, he had supported the racial segregation of universities, trying to keep black students out of white universities. Therefore, despite his being a centrist within the National Party and leading moves against the extreme right wing in 1982, no one really expected him to be any different from his predecessors when he became President in September 1989.

De Klerk was a visionary Afrikaner leader, however, in that he clearly understood that apartheid was in its death throes. He recognised that the only way to move South Africa forward to a peaceful future was through dialogue, and he had the wherewithal to lead his political colleagues and the rest of the country to a new future. As Nelson Mandela described in his book, *Long Walk to Freedom*, 'He was not an ideologue but a pragmatist, a man who saw change as necessary and inevitable.'

In his first speech after becoming leader of the National Party in February 1989, De Klerk called for reform towards a non-racial South Africa and for negotiations about the future. In his inaugural speech as State President, he stated that his government was committed to peace and would negotiate with any other group with a similar commitment. On 15 October 1989 he ensured the unconditional release of Walter Sisulu and seven other former Robben Island prisoners. It was clear that he was committed to changing the status quo at a staggering pace – in his first opening of parliament address on 2 February 1990, he announced the unbanning of the ANC and all other banned organisations, as well as the unconditional release of political prisoners jailed for non-violent activities. He effectively changed the future of the country overnight. On 11 February, Nelson Mandela walked free from Victor Verster prison in Paarl, after almost 28 years behind bars.

'I far prefer being a private citizen in the new South Africa than being President in an old South Africa ... And yes, I remain unashamedly positive about South Africa.'

FW de Klerk
Former South African president

During the negotiations between 1990 and 1994, De Klerk proved to be a very tough political negotiator. He was determined to protect minority rights in the new South Africa. He was accused of not doing enough to quell the political violence that took place over the same period (which was stoked by shadowy 'third force' elements), rather choosing to use it as a negotiating tool. However, he never wavered in his commitment to making a concrete and permanent change in South Africa. When the National Party lost a by-election in Potchefstroom in 1992 to the Conservative Party, he decided to call a referendum of all whites to vote on negotiations and reform. A convincing majority of the vote (69 per cent) went in favour of the government's reform process, and negotiations continued towards a new South Africa characterised, in De Klerk's words, by 'justice, freedom and equality for all'.

It was this commitment to peaceful change that earned FW de Klerk the French Prix du Courage Internationale and a joint UNESCO Houphouet-Boigny Peace Prize in 1992, the Philadelphia Liberty Medal in 1993, and, along with Nelson

Mandela, the 1993 Nobel Peace Prize. In making their award, the Nobel Committee pointed out that these two leaders had looked 'ahead to South African reconciliation instead of back at the deep wounds of the past,' and that the peaceful end of apartheid 'points the way to the peaceful resolution of similar deep-rooted conflicts elsewhere in the world.'

After the first democratic elections in April 1994, FW de Klerk became Executive Deputy President until the National Party withdrew from the government of national unity in June 1996. He retired from active politics in 1997 and has since started the FW de Klerk Foundation, which aims to engage civil society in working towards peace and prosperity in South Africa and other societies divided by culture, ethnicity, race or language.

He, along with the majority of South Africans, has not looked back for a moment since helping to lead South Africa towards freedom and democracy for all, and he continues to speak out in support of the need to be positive about the country. He wrote in *The Citizen* in May 2002: 'I was a very privileged person in the old South Africa. However, despite the many problems that we confront, I far prefer being a private citizen in the new South Africa – based on justice and with an enormously-promising and exciting future – than being President in an old South Africa that could not grant justice to the majority of its people, and that had no future whatsoever. And yes, I remain unashamedly positive about South Africa.' Hear, hear!

Nelson Mandela

Nelson Rolihlahla Mandela is the embodiment of how making the choice to have a positive attitude can affect the lives and futures of others. Despite decades of persecution and imprisonment, he never allowed his overall attitude to become pessimistic, negative or, most importantly, bitter or vengeful. Instead he stuck to his principles, learning constantly and developing the strength and wisdom for which he is now world-renowned.

Madiba (the name of his clan) had an education that was truly Afro-European. After the death of his father, who was chief counsellor to Thembuland's acting paramount chief, Rolihlahla (his given, African name, which means 'pulling the branch of a tree', or more colloquially, 'troublemaker') was brought up in the household of the Thembu chief, Jongintaba. There he was groomed to become an advisor to the chief himself. He was soon sent off to a Methodist school, Clarkebury (where he was given his English name, Nelson), then Healdtown High School and later Fort Hare and Wits University. At these institutions, he developed not only his lifelong passion for education and learning, but also a love of classical European culture such as Shakespeare and Tchaikovsky, and the self-discipline that characterises his lifestyle.

Mandela's learning continued while he was imprisoned on Robben Island. The prison became something of a campus for political prisoners; whenever they could, the prisoners would debate intellectual issues, and later they would help each other out in their studies through the University of South Africa (UNISA). Mandela completed his law degree by correspondence through UNISA and London University during those years. He never stopped learning about people either, always scoping out his captors and trying to work out what made them tick. In this way, he developed a deeper understanding of the Afrikaner mindset that helped tremendously in later negotiations with government, and which fostered the amazing spirit of reconciliation which he displayed after his release. This love of observing, learning and wisdom helps to explain why one of the few things that Mandela is happy to have named after him is schools, as well as the Nelson Mandela Children's Fund to which he pledged one third of his presidential salary for five years.

'I have cherished the ideal of a democratic and free society in which all persons live together in harmony and with equal opportunities ... it is an ideal for which I am prepared to die.'

Nelson Mandela
During the 1963 Rivonia treason trial

Mandela is a man of strict principles, as he showed in his famous speech from the dock during the Rivonia trial in 1963: 'I have fought against white domination and I have fought against black domination. I have cherished the ideal of a democratic and free society in which all persons live together in harmony and with equal opportunities. It is an ideal which I hope to live for and to achieve. But if needs be, it is an ideal for which I am prepared to die.' When the apartheid government offered him his freedom during the 1970s if he agreed to recognise the independence of the Transkei and settle there, he refused because it would legitimise the Bantustan policy. When they again offered to release him in the 1980s if he agreed to renounce violence, he refused again, saying 'Prisoners cannot enter into contracts. Only free men can negotiate.' He had always seen violence against state targets as a sad but necessary consequence of the situation created by apartheid, because 'the government had left us no other choice.' Shortly after his release from prison, he announced on behalf of the ANC leadership the suspension of the armed struggle.

This man of such great wisdom and humility, who gave up the large majority of his life to the struggle for the freedom of all South Africans, was in many ways the successor to Mahatma Gandhi, another lawyer who made it his life's work to fight for non-racialism and the betterment of his people. It is therefore fitting that Nelson Mandela was awarded the Gandhi/King Award for Non-violence in 1999 and The International Gandhi Peace Prize in 2001. These, and a host of other awards, have been added to the joint Nobel Peace Prize awarded to him and FW de Klerk, as well as honorary degrees from more than fifty international institutions of higher learning.

As a strong proponent of *ubuntu*, Mandela has done more to bring the people of this country together since the end of apartheid than anyone else. He has also done more than anyone else to raise South Africa's profile on the world stage, and his wisdom is recognised and respected in the most hallowed halls. When he publicly chastises George W Bush for his sabre-rattling and telephones his father to discuss his behaviour, people do not laugh, they pay attention.

While we hope that South Africa won't have the need for more such examples of reconciliation in the future, we believe that the lessons learnt from the visionary leaders that the country has produced will move us towards a very positive future. We hope that there will be many more leaders, possibly still to be born, who will be shaped by our unique environment and who will become renowned and respected around the world as timeless icons of humanity.

9 Making magic happen

Seeing is believing

Magic happens when we change our perception. There is magic all around us, if we just have the eyes to see it. When something disappears, like apartheid, that's magic; when something changes, like a racist person's attitude, that's magic; when someone pulls a rabbit out of a hat, like Mark Shuttleworth's Afronaut expedition, that's magic; and when someone makes a difference in another's life, like caring for an AIDS orphan, that's magic. One of the things that makes magic happen in South Africa is a healthy sprinkling of positive attitude.

Hopefully we have convinced you by now, that being positive is not the same as going into denial. Rather there are two basic ingredients to being positive. The first is to recognise that our pessimistic views are skewed by unbalanced media reporting. We have to remember that our mental state is determined by what we focus on. It's not that the media is lying; it's just that it is painting a picture of the world and South Africa that is highly selective. The media often appears to patch together a collage, using bits and pieces of real events, most of which happen to be dark, disturbing and thus dramatic. We need to start exposing ourselves to more of the positive news stories, just to get a more balanced perspective of what is really going on around us.

The second aspect to being positive is to recognise that our attitude influences the world around us, for better or for worse. The neutral scientist in the white coat is a myth; he or she does not exist. The observer and the observed are not separate; they are always inextricably linked. Everything we think, or believe, or value, changes the world around us. It even affects our physical health. Attitudes are like lenses that colour what we see; like yeast in bread, a positive attitude can have a leavening effect – on a family, a business, or even a nation.

This is not a philosophical point or theoretical stance. Optimism comes from actively engaging with life's challenges. We know that living in South Africa is no pleasure-boat cruise for anyone – neither the wealthy executive living in fear of being hijacked, nor the street vendor struggling to get food on the table each day. Living in South Africa is a challenge, but that fact in itself creates a set of amazing opportunities.

This is also the underlying premise of internationally-renowned psychiatrist Victor Frankl. Frankl endured unspeakable horror in Nazi death camps, yet emerged with a deep understanding of human behaviour, which he translated into a technique called logotherapy. At its core is the belief that humans' primary motivational force is their search for meaning. He summarises this philosophy in his remarkable auto-biographical book, *Man's Search for Meaning*. Meaning, he says, can be found anywhere, but it is most often associated with overcoming hardships or pursuing a dream. In other words, meaning is created when we respond to challenges or engage with a vision of a better future.

'Magic starts with a state of mind, a way of thinking. Before the practical tools and techniques can be of use, we each have to discover the internal sources of our own stories.'

Marilyn Ferguson
in **Pragmagic**

Frankl's ideas may help to explain the existential crisis being experienced by many people caught up in the 'rat race' of Western culture. Ironically, once you no longer have to worry about material comforts, you begin to wonder whether your life is really worthwhile – are you making a difference in the world? Well, there is certainly no shortage of challenges in South Africa, and the vision of our country as an example for the world to learn from is a compelling dream to hold onto. Could it be that it is easier to live a meaningful life in South Africa than anywhere else in the world?

Closely tied to magic and dreams is the notion of myths, which should not be confused with the contemporary use of the word to mean 'untruths'. Joseph Campbell, perhaps the greatest-ever scholar of mythology, suggests that 'it has always been the prime function of mythology and rite to supply the symbols that carry the human spirit forward, in counteraction to those other constant human fantasies that tend to tie it back.'

Like Frankl, Campbell's theories rest on psychiatrist Carl Jung's notion of archetypes, or patterns of collective consciousness, which are stories that we as humans constantly tap into and identify with. There are numerous myths that South Africans can use to create our positive future – the triumph of good over evil, the poor person's rise from rags to riches, or the genius heretic that revolutionises the world.

The science of optimism

Pessimism is a self-fulfilling prophecy – as is being positive. Martin Seligman, author of *Learned Optimism*, says that people's responses to the world are determined largely by the way they explain things to themselves. Optimists always see a positive spin-off, no matter what the situation is, while pessimists have a self-explanatory style that casts a shadow over everything. As Mike Lipkin and Reg Lascaris write in *Fire & Water*, 'Truly effective people do not allow what is going on around them to dictate their inner state … They carry their own weather within because they know that everything that happens to them has value.'

Optimism is an acquired skill. It is not about denial, or bluffing yourself. It is about being more effective in life. Typically, those who are actively involved in doing something about the problems around them are more optimistic. This is ironic, since they probably know more than most just how bad things really are. In South Africa, this is often the case with people doing work in communities for churches, NGOs and other organisations. The difference is that they also know how much constructive work is being done to tackle the issues. They are aware of all the small success stories that never make the news headlines. They have personal evidence that keeping a positive attitude and engaging in constructive action, especially in the most dire of circumstances, helps to turn situations around.

Those who have learned to turn every circumstance into a potential opportunity – to grow personally or to make a difference – have become our most successful and inspiring leaders, in every field. This is not a secret. There are whole libraries of books dedicated to the theme of becoming more effective by realising the power of our perceptions and attitudes, combined with constructive action. These range from Norman Vincent Peale's classic, *The Power of Positive Thinking*, to numerous others like *Pray and Grow Rich* (Richard Gaylord Briley), *The Dynamic Laws of Prosperity* (Catherine Ponder), *The Seven Habits of Highly Effective People* (Stephen Covey), *Awaken the Giant Within* (Antony Robins), and *The Magic of Thinking Big* (David Schwartz), to mention but a few.

If that all sounds a bit too academic though, just think of sport. How often haven't we shouted at our sports heroes on the television to keep their chins up? Athletes, perhaps more than most, know the importance of positive attitude. They hire sports psychologists to coach them on how to visualise the outcome they desire, how to practise their ideal performances mentally, how to rebound from set-backs, to stay focussed on the goal and never to give up, no matter how impossible the task may seem at the time.

In addition to visualisation, others propose the use of positive affirmations – statements of intent or achievement that are repeated frequently, whether by chanting them or writing them down daily. And in case you think that sounds a bit too much like New-Age mumbo jumbo, there are some pretty successful people who claim it works, like Scott Adams, creator of the international run-away hit cartoon, *Dilbert*. What are your positive affirmations for the country and for your role in it? Why not try writing down a few right now – it won't cost you anything, or harm anyone, and it may just help to change things for the better.

Lipkin and Lascaris apply all this thinking on the science of optimism to South Africa's recent history and suggest three key actions in *Fire & Water:*

1. See things the way they are – take stock of both the positive and negative attributes of your specific situation in this country;
2. See things the way they can be – don't forecast, backcast. Work back from the future. Look beyond the moment to what can be; and
3. Make things the way they can be – take action. Realise that you have the power to make a difference, because if not you, then who?

The lesson of the starfish

Have you heard the story of the starfish? An old man walking along a beach that was strewn with beached starfish came across a woman who was gently putting them back into the sea. He asked her why she was doing this, since the beach was enormous and she could not possibly return all of them to the sea before they died. 'You cannot possibly make a difference,' he said. As she gently put another starfish in the water the woman replied, 'I made a difference for that one.'

This parable, adapted from the story *The Star Thrower* by Loren Eiseley, was the catalyst for a group of South Africans living in London. They felt that something should be done to help the thousands of children that are being orphaned or affected by the AIDS pandemic. So they began by hosting dinners for their friends, charging the cost of a restaurant meal, and putting the money towards an AIDS charity. Soon the initiative grew beyond their wildest expectations.

Today, the Starfish Charity is a registered charity in England and Wales, with offices and operations in South Africa and supporters all over the world, having raised hundreds of thousands of rands from countless individuals. One of those individuals is Mark Fish, the South African footballer currently based in England, who donated £10 000 to the charity and challenged other South African sportspeople based overseas to better that amount. All donations made to the charity are channelled directly to the supported beneficiaries, while operating costs are funded separately by core sponsors. The Starfish Charity is an inspiring example of how doing something, no matter how small or seemingly insignificant, can make a difference, and even create a ripple effect of unexpected positive consequences.

> **'Never doubt that a small group of thoughtful, committed citizens can change the world. Indeed, it's the only thing that ever has.'**
>
> *Margaret Mead*
> *Social anthropologist*

Another example of a project that is trying to make a big difference through small actions, is Phisa. The acronym stands for 'Peace here in South Africa', but it is also a Xhosa word which means 'to give freely and expect nothing in return'. A group of people of any culture, income level, or political affiliation meets once a month to discuss how they can make a small, positive difference to life in South Africa. Once they have introduced themselves and shared their hopes and dreams for the country, they decide as a group on one area of concern to be addressed that month, for example unemployment. They then decide on one concrete action that each member of the group can undertake to try to make a difference, like hiring someone to do something around the house. Finally, they go away and carry out that agreed action. A very small amount of action to address several very big problems, the idea is simply that small actions can set off a chain of progressively bigger reactions. Rather like the story of the butterfly flapping its wings above the Amazon and, eventually, causing a tornado on the other side of the world. The ambitious aim of the project is to turn South Africa into one of the top ten performing nations in the world by 2020, and to make it a country that truly works for all its people. The project is open to anyone who wishes to make a positive difference in South Africa. To find out more, you can send an e-mail to si.ekin@intekom.co.za.

Saying 'I do'

Apart from getting involved in an organisation like the Starfish Charity or Phisa, there are many things that you as an individual can do to make South Africa a better place. Here is a simple list of things to think about and take action on:

Buy South African

Proudly South African exists to encourage people here and overseas to buy quality South African products that are made by socially-responsible companies. The Proudly South African logo is the easiest way to recognise companies that meet these criteria. Supporting this initiative can only do the local economy good by creating local demand for local goods that use local labour. Look out for the logo and buy local before you buy a comparative imported item.

Sell South Africa

Until now we have allowed foreigners to make up their own minds about South Africa, based on their media's portrayal of the country. Their media has relied in turn on our own, overly-negative media to set the tone, and as a result the overarching issues under the spotlight have been those of crime, HIV/AIDS and Zimbabwe. It is up to us ordinary South Africans to change these perceptions. Whether you are a tourist or businessperson travelling overseas, the owner of a B&B or even someone sitting at a bar, sell South Africa to foreigners at every opportunity you get. Why? Well, partly because there is so much to be proud of. But also because, by encouraging foreigners to visit South Africa, you are promoting trade, investment and tourism, and are thereby helping to make a better country for all of us.

If you come across other South Africans running the country down, don't just sit by. Challenge them and work on undoing the untold damage that they are causing to the country's image, and thus to themselves and their families and friends. Point out how many good things there are about the country. If you need any more positive stories to quote in addition to the ones we have already provided here, visit the South African portal website, www.safrica.info. In fact, why not make it your homepage?

Embrace your Africanness

Recognise that you are African and enjoy it. Take note of the things that make Africa unique, especially those quirky little things, like cows grazing next to a six-lane highway, and enjoy them for how different and special they are. Forget about comparing us to Europe and the USA. Rather look at South Africa and Africa in light of the opportunities that they present. Remember the essence of our South African brand: 'Alive with possibility'.

Get to know your fellow South Africans

All of us need to work together if we are going to create that better future. Always keep in mind the spirit of *ubuntu*, the African principle that a person is only a person through other people. Unfortunately, apartheid separated our peoples and kept us apart for so long that now we don't really know very much about each other. Overcome these false divisions between our cultures by talking to each other openly and finding out more about other cultures. Go out on a limb and invite people around for dinner; you'll be amazed how much more you have in common than you think. It is only by knowing each other that we can learn respect and tolerance, which are vital if we are to go forward into the future hand-in-hand.

Become a South African tourist

We have talked about South Africa as a world in one country. Yet there are so many of us who have not visited even a fraction of our own country or the countries around us. If you are looking to go travelling, rather spend your rands locally or in surrounding countries, where your money will still go a long way and where there is so much adventure to be had close to home. If you want culture, go to Johannesburg or Cape Town and experience some of our own theatre, music and art. If you want to go skiing, try the Maluti mountains in winter. And if it's tropical fish you want to see, go diving in Sodwana Bay. Get out there and enjoy it. Learn to love the land in which we live.

Smile and acknowledge

It is truly amazing how much a smile will do to build a nation. For so long South Africans were pitted against each other, and we still so often display elements of mistrust, bitterness, stifled anger, arrogance and general unpleasantness towards each other. Smiles go so far in cutting through all of that. Try forcing yourself to smile from the first moment you interact with someone every day, a security guard at the gate of an office block for example, whether you actually feel like it or not. The positive reaction that you get from a person when you smile at them and they don't expect it is so uplifting that it will make you want to smile again. Then take it one step further and actively acknowledge that person by greeting them and thanking them for the job that they are doing, helping to build their self-esteem in the process. Practise this smiling and acknowledging always – if someone thrusts plastic coat hangers in your face at a traffic light, don't react angrily; smile and say that you really don't need any right now but if you do in the future then you will come back. By acknowledging each other in a positive manner, we take steps towards making this a better country.

Support positive initiatives

If you have enough money to buy this book, then you probably have enough money to buy the monthly *Big Issue* magazine sold by homeless people. (It is, incidentally, a very good read.) There are plenty of positive initiatives like the *Big Issue* that need your support to help those less fortunate than yourself. Let's not wait in vain for the national lottery to solve our problems. Look out for *Homeless News* and others, which create employment and go some way towards making a better life for your fellow South Africans.

Remember that the essence of the South African brand is 'Alive with possibility', and the unique gift of African people to the world is the spirit of *ubuntu*.

Towards a can-do, will-do South Africa

This comment, made by John Kotter at the 1996 BMW Innovative Thinking Conference in Cape Town and quoted in *Fire & Water*, captures our message of optimism poetically: 'Youth is not a time of life; it is a state of mind. It is not a matter of rosy cheeks, red lips and supple knees; it is a matter of the will, a quality of the imagination, a vigour of the emotions; it is the freshness of the deep springs of life. Youth means the temperamental predominance of courage over timidity, of the appetite for adventure over the love of ease. This often exists in a man of sixty more than in a boy of twenty. Nobody grows old merely by deserting their youth. We grow old by deserting our ideals. Years may wrinkle the skin, but to give up enthusiasm wrinkles the soul. Worry, fear, self-distrust turns the spirit back into dust. Whether sixty or sixteen, there is in every human being's heart the lure of wonder, the unfailing childlike attitude of what's next, and the joy of the game of living. In the centre of your heart and my heart, there is a radio station; so long as it receives messages of beauty, hope, cheer, courage and power from people and from the infinite, so long are you young. When the aerials are down, and your spirit is covered with snows of cynicism and the ice of pessimism, then you have grown old, even at twenty; but as long as your aerials are up, to catch waves of optimism, there is hope you may die young at eighty.'

We make no secret of the fact that this book is intended as a 'pep-me-up', but its message goes deeper than injecting a temporary burst of optimism. We are calling for a new way of being in South Africa, a change in the way that we see the world and this country's place in it, a belief in the future of our country. We are promoting positivity and pride, not in a superficial way that pumps up the emotions, but in a way that connects with an underlying belief that we have reason to be positive and proud. We *can* live the South African dream. We *can* make it super-cool to be South African. We *can* make our contribution to a renaissance, not just of this continent, but of the world. So, why not start now? Before you put this book down and go on with your busy life, think of just one thing you can do that will make South Africa a better place. Write it down and make an emotional commitment to do it. By doing this, you will become another can-do, will-do, positive South African. *You* will become one of the many reasons we believe in this country, its people and its future. In fact, by reading this book, you have already made a difference. One of many more to come, we are sure.

The Homecoming Revolution

Featured on the next few pages are three ads from the advertising campaign of **The Homecoming Revolution**. This is an initiative of independent advertising agency morrisjones&co and is aimed at ex-pat South Africans living overseas in an effort to convince them to return home.

The launch ads were developed by morrisjones&co with the Vega School of Brand Communications in Sandton and the Funda Fine Art Centre in Soweto. It's thus a truly collaborative project by diverse South Africans.

THOS (The House of Synergy) is partnering with morrisjones&co to send out e-mercials to a huge database of South Africans currently living and working overseas. THOS is also assisting in the construction and management of **The Homecoming Revolution** website.

morrisjones&co are appealing to the private sector to support **The Homecoming Revolution**. Sponsorship packages are available for corporations. If you would like to sponsor, help or enquire about **The Homecoming Revolution,** please e-mail Angel Jones: angel@morrisjones.co.za.

More good news...

Read

Fire & Water by Mike Lipkin and Reg Lascaris (Zebra Press)
Flying with Pride by Denis Beckett (WildNet Africa)
Radical Innovation – South Africans Leading the World by Wolfgang Grulke with Gus Silber (@One Communications)
South Africa: How are you? by Louis Fourie and JP Landman (Futureworld)
South Africa: The Good News edited by Brett Bowes and Steuart Pennington (Terra Nova)

Surf

Brand South Africa: www.safrica.info
Homecoming Revolution www.morrisjones.co.za
International Marketing Council of South Africa: www.imc.org.za
Positively South African: www.positivelysa.co.za
Proudly South African: www.proudlysa.co.za
South African Tourism: www.southafrica.net
Reasons4SA: www.groups.yahoo.com/group/Reasons4SA/files/

Join

Reasons4SA – subscribe for free on www.yahoogroups.com/groups/Reasons4SA or email Reasons4SA-subscribe@yahoo.com

About the authors

Guy Lundy was born and raised in Cape Town, South Africa. He holds a Bachelor of Social Science and a Bachelor of Commerce (Honours in Economics) from the University of Cape Town. He is currently a director of Centric Management, an international management consultancy specialising in the area of Customer Relationship Management (CRM) and has worked as a consultant for a number of international firms, including Dimension Data, Ernst & Young, Oracle, Hermès and the London Stock Exchange. Guy lived, worked and travelled for several years on four continents before finally settling back in Cape Town with his French wife, Christine. He is an active member of Toastmasters International, and is a professional speaker. His personal interests include reading, writing, surfing, cycling and hiking.

Wayne Visser was born in Bulawayo, Zimbabwe and moved to Cape Town, South Africa, in 1978. He holds a Bachelor of Business Science (Honours in Marketing) from the University of Cape Town and a Master of Science (Human Ecology) from the University of Edinburgh, Scotland. He is currently doing full-time PhD research at the University of Nottingham, England, in the area of Corporate Social Responsibility and Sustainable Development. He is also an international advisor for KPMG's sustainability practice in South Africa where, until recently, he was a director. Prior to this he worked in South Africa as a strategy analyst for Gemini Consulting, and as co-founder and coordinator of the South African New Economics (SANE) Foundation. Wayne is co-author (with Clem Sunter) of *Beyond Reasonable Greed* (Human & Rousseau/Tafelberg, 2002). His personal interests include reading, writing, music, nature and exploring the frontiers of human potential. He is married to Kathleen.